THE
RANGITY
TANGO
KIDS

The Rangity Tango Kids with Grandpa and Grandma
Rominger, on their 50th wedding anniversary, 1974

ANGO KIDS

ir

Lorraine Rominger

Untreed
Reads

The Rangity Tango Kids
By Lorraine Rominger

Copyright 2016 by Lorraine Rominger
Cover Copyright 2016 by Untreed Reads Publishing
Cover Design by Ginny Glass and Jim Shubin
All photos ©Rominger Family, except as noted
Cover photo courtesy of Richard Rominger
ISBN-13: 978-1-94544-702-0

Also available in ebook format.
Published by Untreed Reads, LLC
506 Kansas Street, San Francisco, CA 94107
www.untreedreads.com

For Mom & Dad

My parents, Shirley and Don Rominger,
Christmas, 1973

Contents

My parents, Shirley and Don Rominger, on
their wedding day, 1950

Chapter 1

1950

Mom's wedding day was the happiest day of her life, and as I look through the old photo album I can see why.

Mom and Dad were married on August 13, 1950. They were only 20 years old, and very much in love. Mom looked like a fairy princess in her wedding gown. She and her mother went shopping in San Francisco and bought the gown at The Emporium for $100. The off-white dress, made of organza and chiffon with net and lace overlay, had a ruffled-scoop neck with a fitted bodice and waistline, long see-through net sleeves with tiny buttons from the elbow to the wrist, and buttons all the way up the back. The skirt was covered with layers of organza ruffles from the hipline to the floor, one ruffle tier over the next, cascading into a long train behind the dress that fell under the 20-foot, cathedral-length veil she wore attached to a crown made of pearls. Dad had bought her dainty pearl-drop earrings, and her parents had given her a short, silver necklace strewn with pearls that flattered her long, thin neck. Her dark, softly curled hair framed her face.

Dad wore a black tuxedo with a white shirt and white bow tie, and with his dark, thick straight hair, they made the perfect couple — Don and Shirley Rominger. Beaming ear to ear in the photo album they look like two kids holding on to each other for dear life.

Five bridesmaids and five ushers surrounded them on the altar with the priest and two altar boys. They were all flanked by several six-foot candelabras and white baskets full of white lilies and gladiolas. Mom's sister was her maid of honor and Dad's brother was his best man. Each pew end was covered with a huge white bow and tied with ribbon so guests couldn't enter the pews except through the side aisles.

Dad was Catholic and Mom wasn't. Because of church rules in those days, marrying Mom in the Catholic Church was forbidden unless they attended religious classes for months prior to getting married. Dad's mother was a devout Catholic and she might have been happier if Dad had proposed to a good old-fashioned Catholic girl, but Dad's parents liked Mom and everyone knew how much in love my Mom and Dad were. Dad's parents sat in the front pew on the right side of the church, his mother in a black cocktail dress with a white hat and white elbow-length gloves and his dad in a tuxedo, always prim and proper, and very much the devoted couple.

Mom's parents loved my Dad and couldn't have been happier that their daughter was marrying a young, handsome, hard-working farmer. They sat in the front pew on the left side of the church, holding hands, her father in a tuxedo and her mother in a black cocktail dress with a white hat and net over her face with elbow-length white gloves. In the photos, all the women have on gloves; my Mom wore see-through lace gloves as did her bridesmaids, and the women guests wore gloves and hats with their dresses. All the men wore suits and ties. Things were different back then.

Rice bags were passed out in the church, and Mom and Dad were showered with rice as they left. There's a photo of the two altar boys in their suits in front of St. Anthony's Catholic Church sweeping up the rice, which covered the sidewalk, one of them holding a broom and one a dustpan.

The wedding ceremony was followed by a dinner-dance in Cody's Hall, the only place in town large enough to have a reception, which just happened to be owned by Mom's father's brother. The caterer charged one dollar per person, and the buffet table was covered with so much food that I can't see the table top in the photos beneath the array of trays full of salads, vegetables, potatoes, rice, spaghetti, chicken, steak and dinner rolls. Both sets of their parents were bursting with pride standing next to Mom and Dad at the reception in front of the five-tiered wedding cake with a bride and groom on top in the center of a huge heart. It was the perfect night in the small northern California town of Winters. Mom and Dad knew most everyone, and most everyone in town was there.

After the reception, Dad drove Mom to the Claremont Hotel in Berkeley in his 1947 two-door silver Chevy. It was the first stop on their honeymoon. From there, they drove up the coast of California to see the redwoods, then to Seattle and on to Victoria, British Columbia. One might think driving late at night after partying at your wedding reception would be a bad idea, but neither Mom nor Dad drank any alcohol, not even a glass of champagne. They were under age and my parents obeyed the rules. Mom and Dad dated for four years and were both virgins. Mom told me years later that their wedding night at the Claremont Hotel was the first time they had sex, and I believed her.

Me and Mom on my first birthday, 1952

Chapter 2

I grew up on a farm in a white wooden shack with a sky-blue front door.

My Dad's father, Grandpa Rominger, bought the land in 1930, when my Dad was just a baby. The farm was a few miles from the little agricultural town of Winters.

Mom and Dad met at Winters High School in 1946, and although they had gone on a few dates with other people, once they went out together, that was that. When they got married four years later, Dad didn't have a house, so Grandpa gave him the shack that had been built many years before to house the seasonal farmworkers. No one had ever lived in the shack for extended periods of time or taken care of the place, so it was a mess. Mom spent weeks painting and fixing it up. There were rat holes in the floor so Dad cut the tops off tin cans, nailed them over the holes and covered the floor with carpet. The shack may have been a dump, but it was spotless; Mom never stopped cleaning. When Mom and Dad came home from their honeymoon, Dad drove his Chevy up to the wooden gate in front of the white wooden shack and carried Mom up the sidewalk and through the front door.

I was born eleven months later. My Auntie Lona, Mom's sister, came to the house after high school most every day to play with me. She'd sit by my crib and watch me, rub my head, adjust my blanket and move around my room, not so quietly.

"Lona, you have to let her sleep. Stop waking her up," Mom said.

"I just want to play with her," Auntie replied.

"If you don't stop waking her up, I'm not going to let you take care of her," Mom said.

"OK," Auntie said, but she didn't pay any attention to her sister.

When I was several months old, Auntie would dress me in party dresses that she and Momo Cody, Mom and Auntie's mother, bought for me. She put bows in my hair and sat me on a chair in the middle of the living room.

"My girlfriends are coming to see you and I want you to be a good girl. Don't mess up your hair," Auntie said, as she grabbed my hands and put a toy in my lap. "You are my favorite little girl and I want my friends to see how pretty you are. Just sit there and be still."

Being the first grandchild, I was the center of attention. Auntie snapped pictures of me sitting in those frilly, ruffled dresses, my bare legs and feet just reaching the edge of the oversized wooden chair, photos in my family album we still laugh about.

When I was two years old, Mom and Dad brought my sister, Donna, home from the hospital. According to Auntie the first words I said were, "Get dat baby off my bed." I didn't want to share my Mom, Dad nor Auntie with anyone.

Not long after my third birthday, I figured out how to open the front door of the shack. Across the gravel driveway the wheat field was ready to harvest, golden brown and three feet tall. I let myself out the front gate, walked down the driveway and followed the ditch along the field until it narrowed, where I crossed into the wheat. I sat down in the wheat field in my red corduroy overalls and fell asleep.

"Don, I can't find Lorraine, have you seen her? She must have gone out the front door, but I can't find her in the yard. Oh my God," Mom cried, as she ran through the yard. "The front gate is open. You have to find her, Don. There's water in the irrigation ditch. Go look for her," Mom said, in a panic.

Dad drove around the farm looking for me. Mom was beside herself, Auntie was crying and Dad was scared. He drove up and down the lane in his pickup over and over again and by chance looked into the wheat field at the right moment and caught a glimpse of red. He carried me home in his arms, relieved.

"You're going to stay in your room for a week with your sister. You are not allowed to go outside and play, and I don't ever want you to leave the yard by yourself again," Mom said, shaking her finger at me. "You scared us to death. I was afraid something terrible happened to you. Why did you hide in the field?"

"I don't like it here with that baby. She cries," I said.

"This baby is your sister, and she has colic, and it makes her tummy hurt, so she cries," Mom said.

"Fix her tummy and make her stop crying. I don't like her to cry. Don't cry baby. Mommy, make her better," I said.

Donna slept in the bassinet in Mom and Dad's room after that and I got my room back.

On Sundays, I went to mass at St. Anthony's with Dad. Mom dressed me in my party dress, and Dad and I walked out the front door hand in hand. It was our special time together. I loved sitting on Dad's lap during mass, turning the thin pages of his missal. But the pages tore easily, so Dad would put his hand on mine and we'd turn the pages together, slowly.

Dad never missed Sunday mass, no matter what. His mother was religious and lived by her faith and its teachings. My Grandma Rominger always wore dresses and stockings. She wouldn't be caught dead in a pair of pants, especially in church. "Ladies wore dresses, period," she said. A no-nonsense, hard-working woman, Grandma attended mass every morning, taught catechism and raised her children in the same faith.

After church one Sunday morning as Dad and I drove home in his brand new 1954 two-door, sea-green Ford, which he later told me was his favorite car of all time, he decided to show off and go as fast as he could over the narrow, steep bridge, which sent the car and me flying in the air. I hit my head on the roof of the car and landed on the floor on the passenger side. The car came down with a jolt, slamming onto the blacktop, the sound of metal crashing on the hard surface. Dad said we shouldn't tell Mom, it was our little secret, and since we were both OK, what did it matter? I loved to go fast and had been shouting, "Go faster, Daddy, go faster," and since I was partly to blame, I didn't want to get my Daddy in trouble. We didn't say a word until the next day when Mom couldn't drive the car and Dad had to replace the shocks. Mom knew what had happened; she'd been in the car before with Dad coming across the bridge.

Mom went to the Presbyterian church when she was in high school, but religion wasn't a priority in her life like it was in Dad's and she agreed to raise their children as Catholics. As she was getting me ready to go to church with Dad one Sunday, Mom told me she didn't want to miss anything Dad and I did together, and she was coming with us. So she dressed for church in colored gloves, matching high heels and purse, and a beautiful hat with netting— clothes she had bought, she confessed, before they got married, when she had extra spending money. It wasn't long before Mom became a Catholic and Grandma Rominger was tickled pink. Over the years Mom's faith became as unwavering as Dad's. I was raised by the same faith and teachings.

Every night Mom read me a story, lying on my bed. Then we knelt down beside the bed and said our prayers as we looked at the crucifix hanging on the wall. "Father, son, ghost, men," I said.

"Watch me," Mom said. "Put your hand on your forehead like this," and she took my hand in hers, "then on your heart, then on this shoulder, then on the other shoulder, then together, and say, 'In the name of the Father, and of the Son, and of the Holy Ghost, Amen.' Every night we say our prayers to thank God for all he has given us."

I still say those same prayers every night.

Across the back of the shack was a screened-in porch, the largest room in the house and my favorite place. I rode my sky-blue tricycle back and forth, even in the rain as water seeped in through the screens. At the end of the porch the wooden screen door opened onto the fenced-in backyard covered with hard clay dirt that Mom swept with a broom. The old, moss-covered walnut tree in the center was immense, with many branches that not only covered the backyard, but also the house, engulfing it like an oversized octopus.

"We should be thankful for that old walnut tree. It keeps the house cool in the summer," Mom said.

We didn't have an air conditioner, and it was over 100 degrees in the summer. To fall asleep at night, we'd take a shower and run and jump in bed without drying off. It worked! Dad had been doing that since he was a kid. I played under the walnut tree hour after hour with the dogs. Dad loved dogs and we always had a dog that was part of our family growing up on the farm.

"Lorraine, stop eating the dog food. How many times have I told you it will make you sick?" Mom said. I sat on the ground with King and ate out of his pan every time Dad fed him.

"She didn't eat enough to hurt her," Dad said. "She'll live."

King was Dad's German shepherd and King protected me. He was the big brother I wanted and I followed him everywhere, holding his tail. Mom said he never snapped at me, not even once. I was three and rode King like a horse around the backyard, surrounded by the five-foot cyclone fence that kept both of us inside. We were trapped.

"Daddy, can I go to work with you?" I asked.

"When you stop wearing a diaper and go potty on the toilet you can go with your Dad," Mom said.

Dad was not good at changing diapers, but Dad took King to work with him, and I wanted to go too.

"OK, come on, get in the pickup," Dad said, as he opened the door, picked me up and plopped me on the front seat. "I need to check on the irrigators this morning and you can ride with me," Dad said, as King jumped in the back of the pickup.

I stood next to Dad on the seat with my arm around his neck and held on. He grabbed me out of the pickup, jumped across the irrigation ditch with me in his arms and held my hand as we walked down the rows to check the water. As soon as Dad would let go of my hand to start a siphon, I'd slip and fall in the mud; it never failed. Dad and I got in trouble when we got home; Mom just didn't understand how Dad could let me get all muddy.

I wanted Donna to be bigger, like me, so we could play together too. But I had to pull her around because she couldn't keep up.

"How many times have I told you not to drag your sister through the gravel? Her knees are scratched and bleeding. She's just a baby," Mom said.

Trouble followed me when my little sister was around, except when Mom and Dad had parties and my cousins came and I didn't have to play with her. The picnics on the patch of grass in the front yard happened often. There was no way all the family could fit in the shack; it was barely big enough for the four of us.

Mom was pregnant and I asked for a big brother. It didn't cross my mind that I was always going to be the biggest. Five of us in the shack were going to be crowded. Grandma and Grandpa helped Mom and Dad build a new house just across the equipment lot behind the shack, and we moved in before Mom and Dad brought Joe home from the hospital.

Our new house didn't look like a farmhouse at all. It was brand new, built of gray Base-lite concrete bricks with red wooden trim around the windows, red metal rain drains and a red wooden back door.

"Concrete is the best material to build a house. It will keep us cool in the summer and warm in the winter," Dad said, as we walked through our home for the first time.

It was also the cheapest material to build a house with and required the least amount of upkeep. Dad was busy working on the farm, and the last thing he wanted to do was take care of things around the house. Women took care of the house; that's how my parents were raised.

"You kids are lucky," Dad said. "Our new house comes with a pool."

Dad forgot to mention the pool was four feet wide, eight feet long, two feet deep and made of cement. It was a baby pool, and I wasn't a baby any more. I couldn't even dive off the edge without scraping my knees on the bottom.

Donna and I shared a room, which I thought stunk. I had to share everything with my little sister and I had to watch her often because Mom had a new baby. Joe had a room to himself and that didn't seem fair. Sometimes being the oldest wasn't much fun.

Joe was pretty and had lots of dark, curly hair. He was little, and I had to be gentle when I held him. I loved holding him on my lap, kissing his face and stroking his hair. But he wasn't going to be bigger than me, at least not for a long time, I thought.

Dad and Me, on Grandpa's horse, Prince, 1953

Chapter 3

**Our new house was a stone's throw from Grandma and Grandpa
Rominger's traditional three-story farmhouse.**

The covered wooden raised porch that circled the house was the best
place to play. A grand hotel that stood out on the farm like a fort in
the middle of the prairie—that was Grandpa and Grandma's house.

Grandpa Rominger was 6'3", 250 pounds, strong and tough. He
was one big, German farmer and a giant to me. A quiet man of few
words, I felt safe with him. I was his first grandchild and he liked to
hold me on his lap. I liked it too.

Grandpa's horse was named Prince and I got excited every time
I rode across the fields with Grandpa.

"Hold me tighter," Grandpa," I said. "It's a long way down."

"I think you're big enough to ride behind me. Scoot up as close as
you can and put your arms around my waist," Grandpa said.

"My arms aren't long enough." I grabbed his sides and squeezed
as hard as I could. "Grandpa, can I have a horse when I get old like
you?"

"Old, I'm not old, I'm big," he said, with a laugh. "You need to
talk to your Dad about getting a horse of your own."

The minute Grandpa grabbed me under my arms and lowered
me to the ground, I ran into the house.

"Dad, Grandpa said I need to ask you if I can have a horse of my
own."

"When you're big enough to take care of a horse, we'll talk about
you having a horse."

"What does bigger mean? How big do I have to be?"

"I know you want a horse. You have to wait a few more years."

"A few years. I'll be big then, and old, like Grandpa."

"Come here and sit next to me," Dad said, as I nestled up beside him. "I don't think you'll ever be as old as Grandpa. But when you are bigger, I promise we'll talk about getting you a horse."

Aunt Claire rode Grandpa's horse and was an excellent rider. I spent lots of time with my Dad's sisters, Aunt Claire, Aunt Lucille and Aunt Joan. Aunt Claire had long, beautiful dark hair and I wanted to be like her.

"Can I comb your hair, Aunt Claire?" I asked.

We sat by the fireplace while I combed her hair and watched her paint her fingernails with red polish. I called her Vampira and loved her long fingernails, probably because I bit mine so bad they bled.

One evening Donna and I stayed at Grandma's and snuck into Aunt Claire's bedroom and accidentally spilled makeup on her upholstered vanity stool and carpet.

"Girls, what are you doing in here? How many times have I told you not to play with my things," hollered Aunt Claire, as she swatted us both on our bums. "Look at the mess you've made. Now you get out of my room this minute and put my makeup down."

"Aunt Claire," I cried, "how can you be so cruel to me when I love you so much?"

"Well," Donna protested, "that didn't hurt at all. Go ahead. Hit me again. I'm going to tell Grandma you hit us. Come on Lorraine, you crybaby. Let's get out of here."

"I'm sorry, Aunt Claire. Please don't be mad at me," I said, with tears in my eyes.

"You two girls are different as night and day."

"What does that mean?"

"You never mind. I think it's time for bed. Let's have Grandma read your favorite story."

My favorite book was *Jack and Zip* and my second favorite was *The Little Engine That Could*. Grandma read the books to me every time I spent the night at her house, but what I loved most was sitting on her lap. Grandma kept favorite books for each of her grandchildren and Mom bought us every Dr. Seuss book there was. We read them over and over until the pages fell out. *The Cat in the Hat, Horton Hears a Who* and *How the Grinch Stole Christmas* were the ones I remember most.

Donna and I spent evenings with Momo and Popo Cody, our mother's parents, who lived four miles away in Winters. Mom had varicose veins when she was pregnant with Joe and stayed in bed for days at a time. It was a good thing Momo and Popo lived close by so they could babysit and give Mom a break. Mom was always busy cleaning and cooking and taking care of us kids. I remember when I wet the bed and got up in the middle of the night to have her change my sheets. I'd see the light on in the laundry room and she'd be sitting at the mangle, ironing. She ironed everything, even my sheets.

"There's no one I feel safe leaving you with, but your aunts and your grandparents," Mom said.

I grew up knowing the love of two sets of grandparents and four aunties who spent hours playing with me. I had no idea how lucky I was.

Popo and Momo Cody lived in a big dollhouse. It was white stucco with black trim and sat back off the street on a corner lot, the house surrounded by grass that stretched out to the sidewalk running up and down the narrow, tree-lined streets. The grass was bright green and not a weed in it. Donna and I played with Auntie in Momo's garden. We were picking Momo's flowers and putting them in glass canning jars lining the patio when one of the jars dropped.

"Lorraine, what happened? What have you done to yourself?" Auntie shouted. "There's blood everywhere. It's all over your clothes."

"I dropped the jar and cut myself. Am I going to die?"

"Sweetie, you're not going to die. Mom, come out here. Lorraine's bleeding and her hands are covered in blood," Auntie said.

Momo took me to the kitchen and ran my hands under the cold water as I cried, screaming for my Mom.

"You cut your finger pretty bad," Momo said. "Lona, call the doctor's office. She's going to need stitches."

"I don't want to go to the doctor, Momo," I cried, sitting on the kitchen counter as she wrapped my finger with a rag.

"The doctor will fix your finger," Momo said.

"I don't like it here. I want to go home. I want my Mommy."

"Your Mommy is out of town," Auntie said.

"Well then, I'll take my Daddy."

I needed ten stitches at the base of my right index finger that Auntie swore I was going to lose. Momo drove me to the doctor's office in her new pink Thunderbird that I had never ridden in before and held my hand all the way. Momo didn't leave my side. She had the sweetest, calming voice that made everything all right. I don't remember Momo ever raising her voice to me, even when I deserved it. She was such a kind and loving grandmother. Her mother had died when she was only nine, and she grew up taking care of her brothers and sisters.

Popo ran his brother's convenience store and gas station just outside Winters. The store was a gathering place for his friends and customers who hung out at the beer counter after work. The back room was full of pinball machines and a tournament-length shuffleboard against one wall, where Donna and I loved to play.

"Come on, let's play shuffleboard. I'm red and you're blue," I said, as we ran into the back room.

"You're always red," Donna said.

"Well then, you can be red and I'll be blue."

"It doesn't matter anyway. It's not fair. You always win because you're bigger and older than I am. Plus you're bossy and always telling me what to do. Someday I'm going to... kick your butt."

"That's not very nice. I'm trying to help you like Grandpa helps me, but you're such a hard head you think you know everything."

"I do know everything," Donna said. My sister was a tough cookie.

Popo brought the money home from the store in a large wad with a rubber band around it. Donna and I sat on the floor in his living room counting the money.

"Popo, you're rich. Look at all your money," I said, as I counted 100 one-dollar bills one at a time.

In the middle of the living room on the coffee table sat a green, two-foot-long, hollow ceramic replica of a crocodile, full of pennies. Donna and I counted the dollar bills and pennies over and over for what seemed like hours. Momo gave me the crocodile and I kept it.

UNION SCHOOL - 1936
TOP ROW, L TO R: JOE LAWRENCE, DON ROMINGER, RICH ROMINGER. 2nd ROW: HARRY FREDERICKS, ERELDA FAWCETT, ADELINE LAWRENCE, VIRGINIA NEEL, ?, LILLIAN RUSSELL, MANDRED CHAPMAN. FRONT ROW: MARJORIE APPLE, DWAINE PARTAIN

Dad and his brother, Richard, at Union School,
top center, 1936

Chapter 4

When I was six, I started first grade in a one-room schoolhouse, the very same school my Dad attended.

Union School had been named after Union Slough, where the school was originally built. But the slough flooded every year and so did the school. The school district decided to move the building to the corner of a field owned by my Grandpa Rominger where it would be centrally located between the families out in the country so their kids could walk to school. Union School was now two miles up Road 29 from our house and I counted the days all summer waiting for school to begin. I was excited as Mom drove me to school the first day. She opened the door as I jumped out and ran to the playground.

"Don't forget your lunch," she said, following me and handing me the brown paper bag with my name written on it in black.

Big cement steps led to the green door of the white wooden school with a 40-foot clock tower attached to the building at the front door. The windows covering the west side of the schoolhouse were trimmed in green with a green canvas awning operated by a hand crank to cover the windows during the heat of the day. Two-foot-high green letters painted above the door read UNION SCHOOL.

Mrs. Metzger was my first teacher. There were twenty-three students, grades one through eight. Each of us sat at a wooden desk with an attached chair, lined up neatly in several rows, with a desktop that pushed straight up, storing our books, papers and pencils inside. All of us were assigned a wooden hook to hang our coats on and a small wooden shelf with our name for our lunch. A 20-foot-long green chalkboard covered the wall where Mrs. Metzger stood in front of the class and wrote our assignments. The tray beneath the chalkboard was crowded with white chalk and black felt hand erasers. The powder from the chalk filled the tray and covered my clothes after it was my turn to erase the board. The big kids helped the little kids. There were twin girls in third grade—I had never seen twins before—and they were nice to me. The class was half boys and half girls, whites and Mexicans, and one teacher. We were all one and the same inside the one-room schoolhouse.

Every recess and lunch hour we played in the schoolyard. The older kids treated me like I was their little sister and I loved having big kids around who watched out for me. A tetherball pole, a set of monkey bars, a merry-go-round, a teeter-totter and a double set of swings made of steel filled the schoolyard. The schoolhouse sat in the middle of an acre, surrounded by a playground covered in dirt with a three-foot wire fence and pine trees lining the edges. At first I had a hard time keeping up with the big kids, but as I got older I could grab the monkey bars and make it all the way to the other side.

Most of the time we played our favorite game called Horses, a game of tag with two teams, and the fastest runners had the biggest advantage.

"Earl, I want to be on your team. Pick me," I said, standing in line with the kids.

"You're the littlest, just wait," he answered, but he never picked me. I was heartbroken. Earl was the most handsome boy I had ever seen and I had a crush on him.

When I started third grade, Donna came to Union School with my cousin Rick, Uncle Richards's oldest son. Uncle Richard was my Dad's only brother and the oldest of the five siblings. I watched out for my little sister and cousin, just as the big kids watched out for me.

We started riding our bikes to school that year, the same year the new neighbor kids came to Union School. Ryan and his family moved into the farmhouse down the road from us and Ryan was a big bully. He had to be first to reach the schoolyard on his bike every morning. I wanted to beat him so bad and I tried and tried, but I never did.

The north wind blew six months out of the year and it blew hard. "I hate riding my bike to school in the north wind, Mom. I pedal and pedal and pedal faster and it feels like I'm standing still. Ryan races every morning and he's bigger than me. He always wins."

20

When Dad was little and first went to Union School in 1935, there was no electricity, no heat and no running water in the schoolhouse. They used a wood stove for heat and Dad said some days during the winter it was so dark inside they could barely see to read. Sometimes he rode his horse to school, and once in a while on weekends Grandma would let him ride the horse to go visit his friends, but Dad's friends lived far away so he spent most of his time playing with his brother and sisters. He only got to go see his friends on special occasions. His Mom and Dad would take the horse and buggy to school events in the evening, and it was pitch black when the event was over, but Dad said the horses always knew the way home.

On Halloween, our parents sponsored a treasure hunt. We didn't get to trick-or-treat living in the country because houses were miles apart. Everyone in school dressed up, and wore a costume with a mask, and sometimes I didn't know who was who. My favorite costume was Little Red Riding Hood. It didn't matter what we wanted to be, Mom was good at making things, and she never said no. I was scared in the dark schoolyard looking for clues with our flashlights, spooking each other, hunting for the buried treasure. I never found that darn treasure once, but I loved the hunt.

The annual talent show took place in the spring. Even though my dance teacher told Mom I was too tall and uncoordinated for my age to be a ballerina, I loved to dance.

"Mom, can you make me a fairy costume for the talent show? I'm dancing with two girls in my class and we're going to be fairies. I need a special fairy dress."

We practiced every day and Mom spent weeks sewing our dresses that looked exactly like knee-length ballet tutus. So what if my teacher said I'd never be a ballerina, I was going to look like one. The royal blue tutu was covered with silver sparkly stars on the net skirt and Mom made silver, sparkly crowns with silver wands, and we wore silver sparkly ballet slippers.

"Mom, this is perfect. It's what I wanted. Even if I don't win, I'll have the best costume."

The dance was a disaster. I was nervous and forgot the routine, and when I looked over at the other girls we were all doing different steps. I tripped twice and almost fell. When I looked at Mom and Dad sitting in the audience, they were both smiling and clapping. Mom winked, and Dad mouthed, "Don't stop."

I made up steps as the music played and bowed like a fairy princess at the end. As I ran backstage, Dad was there. "I'm proud of you. You never gave up. That's my girl," as he put his arms around me.

"I tripped and forgot the steps. My teacher's right, I don't think I'm ever going to be a ballerina."

"Who cares? You're good at other things, and all that's important is that you finished. You didn't give up."

My Dad never started anything he didn't finish.

We won best costume in the show. Mom was thrilled; me too. I saved the royal blue tutu with silver stars.

When school was out, Donna and I and our cousins, Rick and Charlie, took swimming lessons at the city pool. Charlie was just a year younger than Rick and the four of us played together all summer. I was the tallest and both Donna and I had dark brown hair with a pixie cut, but Rick and Charlie were towheads and the chlorine in the water at the swimming pool turned their long blond hair green.

"I think you kids should join the swim team," Dad said. "You're good swimmers. Being on a team is a great way to learn sportsmanship—how to win and how to lose."

We joined the team. Bobbie Greenwood was our coach and all the kids looked up to her. I did what she told me to do because I wanted to be the best.

"Remember," Dad said, "it's not whether you win or lose, it's how you play the game." He paused. "But as far as I'm concerned you play to win, otherwise what's the point."

Dad was competitive and wanted to be the best at whatever he did and it rubbed off on us. We practiced every morning during the week and had a swim meet every weekend the first half of summer.

Mom and Aunt Evelyne, Uncle Richard's wife, took turns taking us to town for practice.

"Where is she?" I asked. "We're going to be late again," as I paced in front of the kitchen window.

Just as practice was starting, Aunt Evelyne bombed up in her white Ford station wagon and screeched to a halt. We ran out and piled in the car, our towels dragging behind, stuck in the closed door.

On Friday afternoons Mom made us take a nap before the swim meet and I couldn't sleep in the middle of the afternoon with the sun shining in the bedroom. Mom insisted we stay in bed for two hours whether we fell asleep or not, and she made us eat steak and potatoes to give us energy. She did everything she could to help us and never missed a meet.

"Where's Dad, do you see him?" I asked, standing by Donna at the end of the pool. "Is he here yet?"

Dad worked late in the summer because of harvest, but as we got on the starting blocks for our first race, he'd show up in the nick of time in his filthy short-sleeve work shirt, rolled-up Levis, work boots and cowboy hat.

"There he is. He made it. I knew he would." I wanted Dad to be proud of me.

"Dad, did you see me race?" I asked, as I ran to him after the finish.

"Great job. Keep practicing and next time you'll win." Nothing was good enough for Dad other than first.

When the swim season was finished, Donna and I had a shoebox full of blue, red and white ribbons. We both swam freestyle, breaststroke and relay, and Donna swam butterfly, but I was crappy at butterfly and swam backstroke. Good thing Donna and I were in different age groups and I didn't have to swim against my sister. It could have been embarrassing.

My first summer job on the farm was picking up black walnuts. I was seven. There were hundreds of trees on the farm that grew along the ditches. Dad helped me pick the walnuts off the ground, put them in a big plastic bucket and dump them in a gunnysack. He came back in a couple of hours to check on me.

"Let's see, how many sacks do you have? Ten sacks, that's ten dollars," Dad said.

One dollar a sack, I thought I was rich.

"I'm going to show you how to sew up the sack," he said, as he gave me a six-inch-long steel needle and a spool of string. "Watch me. You thread the needle, hook it on the side of the sack with a knot, roll the top of the sack over and sew it together like this. Now you try it."

I did it until I got it right. Dad spent hours teaching me to do things and he was an excellent teacher. I raced to the shop in the morning, got my bucket and walked along the ditch from tree to tree.

"No one can pick walnuts faster than you can," Dad said. "You are going to make a great farmer someday."

It was my first paying job and I loved making my own money. At the end of summer, Dad took me to town and I opened a savings account at the local bank and put $35 in my account. I watched the teller write in the amount and stamp the date in my little brown savings book. I kept that savings book in my desk drawer in my bedroom and would frequently check on it just to make sure it was there.

Dad grew hundreds of acres of barley on the rolling hills, and after the grain was planted we prayed for rain, the only source of water in the hills. Within a few months, all we saw for miles was green rolling hills, three-foot-tall grain swaying in the wind, dotted with yellow mustard weeds. Dad hated yellow mustard in his grain field and we spent hours together walking through the fields cutting mustard. It was a crappy job, but he paid me two dollars an hour.

Mom and Dad brought Dan home from the hospital the summer I turned nine. Joe was four, and now I had two baby brothers to help take care of. Dan had straight, light brown hair and never cried. Mom was sick during her pregnancy with Dan and almost ended up in the hospital.

"I know you're only nine, sweetie, but your Mom doesn't feel good and I need you to be a big girl and help her," Dad said. "Do you think you can do that?"

"Sure, Dad. I'll help Mom, don't worry."

"Mom, I can watch Donna and Joe. I know you don't feel good."

Being the oldest, I watched my sister and brother. I didn't like it much when I was younger because Mom said I was too rough and she was always correcting me. But as I got older Mom told me how much she appreciated my help, and that made me feel special.

When I started fourth grade, we got a new teacher at Union School named Miss Olson, and she was strict.

I came home from school and Mom said, "What are those marks on your face?"

"Miss Olson picks on me. She's not fair. The other kids talk and I'm the one who gets in trouble. She puts wide, brown tape on my mouth and everyone laughs at me."

I marched into the house a few times a week with red lines in a square around my mouth.

"You better stop talking or you're going to have that red square around your mouth all year," Mom said.

"Lorraine talks all the time," Donna said.

"You tattletale," I said. "I do not talk all the time. That's not true."

"I'd say you're cruisin' for a bruisin'," Dad said. "You need to behave in school. I'll go talk to Miss Olson and find out for myself what's going on."

"No, Dad. The kids will give me a hard time."

"You're the oldest and need to set a good example for your sister. She looks up to you," Dad said.

The last thing I wanted was Mom and Dad going to school and talking to my teacher. I would never hear the end of it. Thank goodness I talked him out of it.

Once in a while Mom went shopping after school and left us home with Dad in charge. The hallway in our house was 30 feet long and connected the kitchen, living room and dining room to the bedrooms and bathrooms at the opposite end of the house. The hallway was covered with gray linoleum and was slippery because Mom never stopped waxing the floors. Donna and I closed all the doors to the bedrooms and bathrooms, put on our socks and ran and slid from one end of the hallway to the other.

"It's my turn," Joe said.

"No, it's my turn," Donna replied.

"No, it's my turn," I said, as we screamed and pushed one another.

"Dad, Lorraine is pushing me and I didn't get my turn," Joe hollered.

"I don't want to hear another word from you kids," Dad said, from his chair in the den reading his hunting magazine. "Don't come in here unless one of you is bleeding."

Dad was boss and had a big bark and no bite. He never raised a hand to spank us, he just sent us to our room. Dad expected more from me because I was the oldest and he taught me to do things before he taught my sister and brothers. He taught me guy things and I thought he would have been happier if I was a boy. Mom convinced me he taught me guy things only because he was a guy and those were the things he knew.

"I think it's time you learn to drive," Dad said, one afternoon.

Off we went in Dad's pickup truck with his rifle in the gun rack inside of the cab's back window and me sitting between his legs with my hands on the steering wheel. My feet weren't quite long enough to touch the gas and brake, so I steered and Dad hollered.

"To the left, to the left. Don't turn the wheel so much," Dad said, as he grabbed the wheel and turned it in the opposite direction. "You're running off the road. What are you doing? Pay attention. Turn the wheel just a little, like this."

Miles and miles of dirt roads on the farm ran through the fields. Every field had an access road to get the equipment in and out to work the ground and Dad knew those roads like the back of his hands. So did I before long. Dad knew his land, the farms next to his, who owned them and where his neighbors came from.

"Daddy, look, there's a deer," I said, pointing. "It's a fawn, it has white spots."

Dad taught me to recognize every animal in the field: deer, coyote, squirrel, raccoon, possum, jackrabbit, skunk, turkey, eagle, hawk, pheasant, quail, dove and rattlesnake. I loved them all, except the snakes. I'm not sure all of us kids ever realized how much knowledge we soaked up about animals, birds, crops and trees by just living on a simple farm. Mom served for supper the animals Dad shot, except the varmints that ate his crops, like the rabbits and squirrels and crows.

"Daddy, why are we stopping?" It was a hot, sunny day.

"Look up ahead. See that snake coiled in the middle of the road? It's a rattler. Move over and stay in the truck."

Dad fired his rifle, picked up the dead snake and brought it back to the pickup.

"Daddy, you blew his head off. What are those?"

"Those are rattles. Hear that noise they make?" he asked, as he shook the rattles in front of my face. "That's the noise you hear if you get too close to a rattlesnake and he's about to strike. Stay clear of those buggars. Their bite is poisonous and will make you sick if it doesn't kill you. That's a keeper. Count the rattles."

"Thirteen," I said, as Dad set the rattles on the dashboard.

Every time Dad killed a rattler, he cut off the rattles and his collection slid around on the dashboard. Thirteen rattles remains the most he ever cut off any rattlesnake.

We never saw a rattlesnake in the yard, but many mornings our yard was swarming with wild turkeys, sometimes as many as thirty. Dad woke us up so we could sneak a peek, but most of the time we could hear them clucking outside our bedroom window. For years, Dad threatened to shoot one and serve it for Thanksgiving, but he never did. Mom said wild turkeys tasted too gamey no matter how long she soaked them in milk and ketchup and lemon juice.

During summers on the farm we had the biggest playground in the world at our back door. Donna, Joe, Dan and I spent the days playing with our cousins, Rick, Charlie, Ruth and Bruce. Ruth and Bruce had been born between the birth of my two brothers; Dan was the baby of the group and the sweetest of us all. We tied round cardboard tops from baling-wire boxes to the back guard of our bikes with twine and chased each other to try and run over the box tops and break the twine. The last one of us with the box top dragging was the winner. Problem was the boys played rough and crashed into us girls on purpose and one of us usually went home in tears, except Donna. Whenever we crashed our bikes and scraped our knees or elbows, Dad put Merthiolate, a dark-red topical antiseptic, on our cuts. He applied it straight from the little bottle with a glass applicator, and insisted it killed the germs and would make it all better. But it burned like heck.

"Just blow and keep blowing, it'll be fine," Dad said. "The sting only lasts for a minute."

We were forever getting thorns and splinters in our fingers and thumbs and Dad would take us in the kitchen and cut them out with his sharp little pocket knife, squeezing our outstretched hand in his while we turned away, hollering. Then he'd zap the tiny cut with that red stuff and it burned for a minute while he blew on it. There were times Mom ran into the kitchen and said she thought one of us was dying we were screaming so loud.

Rick watched out for his brothers and sister the same way I watched out for mine. Charlie was bossy and Bruce was crazy and Joe wanted to win at everything. We were a rowdy bunch of kids, but we didn't get in much trouble. We'd take off in the morning and play for hours without a care—safe on the farm in our own little world.

We drank out of the garden hose in the yard and never worried about getting sick. We got on our bikes on Saturday morning and didn't come home until supper without Mom worrying about where we were or whether people were hurting us. We never wore bike helmets. We sat in the front seat of the car with Mom and had never heard of kid car seats. We drank milk straight from the cow and never thought about bacteria. We ate unwashed fruit off the vine and never worried about the pesticides Dad had sprayed on them. We never locked our doors at night and people thought we were crazy. But Dad had faith in people, which filled us all with the same faith.

A few years after Mom and Dad built the new house, they poured a three-foot-wide sidewalk around the house and I spent hours roller skating in circles. Sometimes Donna skated with me, but I was faster than she was and she'd get mad and quit. We had metal skates with braces that attached to the hard soles of our shoes and we tightened the skates using a metal skate key that we wore around our necks. Dad was constantly reminding me not to leave my key lying around so he put it on a string.

Donna and I loved to play jacks and pick-up-sticks. We'd sit on the linoleum floor in the hallway trying to beat each other over and over again, and Mom would have to holler at us and tell us it was time to go to bed. We each had a set of jacks that came in a leather pouch with one red rubber ball and ten multicolored jacks. Dad taught Donna and me to play checkers and I usually won. Donna complained it was only because I was the oldest and had played more times than she had. So I taught Joe and Dan to play and it wasn't long before Joe beat me every time.

Dad repaired the farm equipment when it broke down and we helped by gathering pieces of scrap metal from the junk pile. The shop where Dad and the mechanics worked on the equipment was a huge barn made of corrugated metal. There were rows and rows of nuts and bolts and screws and washers on wooden box shelves, one on top of the other covering one of the shop walls. A metal press and sieve to make parts for the tractors, a lathe to smooth the metal pieces together tightly and steel containers full of tools covered the shop floor. As kids, we weren't allowed inside the shop without Dad or Grandpa.

Grandpa used the lathe to make all his daughters, daughters-in-law and granddaughters candlesticks for wedding gifts. I don't mean just any old candlesticks, but adjustable, geometric, solid brass candlesticks—family heirlooms. I couldn't wait until I was old enough to be given a pair of candlesticks made by Grandpa.

"Don't touch that," Dad said, in a stern tone. "You kids need to be careful, you can get hurt on this stuff. Don't look at that, it will burn your eyes." Sparks flew from the welder and red-hot pieces of metal dropped on the cement. "It can blind you. Stand back."

Dad paid me to clean the shop. I swept the floor and organized the nuts and bolts and tools after the men went home at night. One of the farmworkers, Mr. Heil, worked in the shop and had come from Hungary looking for work. Grandpa hired him to fix things on the farm. Mr. Heil and his wife lived in our old shack and had two kids, Frank and Julie, a few years older than us. Frank worked on the farm too, but Mrs. Heil and Julie pretty much stayed to themselves and Dad said it was because they barely got out of Hungary alive and were afraid to leave the shack. I tried to talk to them when I saw them on the farm, but they seemed leery of me and I felt bad for them. But Mr. Heil became part of our family. He was a large man, tall and robust, with a mustache. When he first came to the farm he was quiet and didn't say much, but as we got to know him and he got to know us, it was like he had worked on the farm forever. He could fix anything and Dad said he was the best handyman he had ever seen. Plus, Mr. Heil was always organizing things in the shop and on the farm and cleaning up everyone's messes.

"Wait until you see what Mr. Heil built you kids," Dad said.

"Daddy, I've never seen anything like it," I said, standing at the bottom of the tree looking up the wooden steps on the trunk.

"Well, go ahead. Climb up and check it out."

The tree fort was two stories high. Ladder-like steps on the trunk led to the first landing that circled the big black walnut with a carved wooden machine gun attached to the top of the rail on a swivel so we could kill the bad guys that attacked us. Smaller steps led higher up the trunk to a tower with a landing surrounded by a tall rail. A thick rope hung from the tree fort in the middle of the ditch that we swung on to cross to the other side.

Mr. Heil's tree fort was a smashing success. The eight of us spent hours playing in the tree fort, swimming in the ditch and floating on inner tubes. Lots of times Mom would make us picnics and we had parties in the fort and spent the night in our sleeping bags. But there were five boys and three of us girls, and lots of times the boys hogged the fort and didn't want us girls around.

My horse, Lady, and her new colt, Bay Boy, 1962

Chapter 5

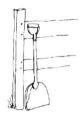

Donna and I had chores to do every day.

"Girls, it's time to clean your room," Mom said. "Get the vacuum and the dust rags."

"Mom, I have homework," Donna said.

"You know Thursday is the day you girls clean your room. You can do your homework later. Donna you dust, Lorraine you vacuum. The sooner you get started, the sooner you'll be finished," she said, as she rolled the vacuum into our bedroom.

There was no getting out of it. Mom was a neat freak and insisted we clean our room every Thursday. Our room was painted bubble-gum pink with twin beds covered in purple and pink satin-striped bedspreads; a hardwood floor with pink rugs; and white, antique-stained furniture. We both had a V-shaped corner desk with a hanging swag lamp covered in pieces of oyster shells and a dresser and bookcases that lined the walls. There was a place for everything—in the drawer, on the shelf, in the closet—so nothing was left sitting around.

Donna and I had a collection of original Barbie dolls that filled our room and we spent hours playing with them, some with short hair and some with long blond ponytails. Our Barbie had a pink Corvette, an apartment with furniture, a fashion store, multiple outfits and very special clothes that Momo Cody hand crocheted—coats, sweaters, skirts, dresses, hats and even scarves. But every Thursday we had to put the Barbies away in their boxes and I never understood the point in that, because the next day the Barbies were everywhere, with their apartments set up again on the floor in the middle of our room.

Donna and I both learned to clean house. Donna learned to cook and I learned to garden. Mom was patient and didn't expect us to get it perfect the first time, like Dad. But my sister disappeared when it was time to do her part.

"Donna, where are you going?"

"I have to go to the bathroom," she'd say, as she walked out of the bedroom. She spent hours on the toilet.

It was her favorite trick. I ended up dusting and vacuuming, but I didn't care. I wanted to finish before Mom came to check the room, which she always did.

After dinner, Donna and I were in charge of clearing the table and doing the dishes. We ate together as a family every evening; it was a ritual in our house. Mom and Dad believed in the importance of doing things together as a family.

"I got an *A* on my math test today," Donna said.

"Good job, honey," Mom said.

"That's my girl," Dad said, as he picked up his glass to make a toast, the ice clinking against the sides of the half-full glass of water.

"I raked all the leaves in the front yard after school Dad," I said.

"I know you did. I saw the yard when I came home. You're the best gardener around," he said, as he raised his glass again.

"What did you boys do at school today?" Mom asked.

"School is boring and I don't like my teacher. I don't understand why I have to go to school," Joe said.

"You can work with me in the fields," Dad interrupted. "I'll get you up at 5 a.m. tomorrow. Pack your lunch and I'll drop you off in the grain field at the South-60. You can walk the hills and cut the mustard and I'll come back and pick you up at supper time," Dad said.

34

"The South-60? That's way back in the foothills. Are you going to leave me there all day by myself?" Joe asked, with a puzzled look on his face.

"You can go to school or you can work in the field."

"That's not fair, Dad. I don't spend the whole day in school."

"You can go to school or you can work in the field. Your choice."

"I'll go to school then, but I'm still gonna be bored."

"Good. That's settled," Dad said, as he picked up his fork and continued eating.

The Formica kitchen table was rectangular and Dad sat at the head. Mom sat next to him on one side and Donna sat next to Mom. Joe and Dan sat opposite Mom and Donna on a bench attached to the wall and I sat at the opposite end of the table. I was the oldest so I got to pick my seat first and I liked sitting opposite Dad.

Being raised on a farm, we ate meat and dairy every day because we had our own cows and chickens. Dad said as long as we worked hard and got lots of exercise, we could eat what we wanted. Dad grew vegetables and we ate vegetables every night too.

"This is a hate-able dinner," Joe said.

"Joseph, apologize to your mother and eat your dinner," Dad said.

Whenever Joe didn't want to eat something, he'd tell Mom the dinner was hate-able, Dan too. When Donna and I cleared the table, under Dan's plate was a circle of green peas. He wasn't fooling anyone, but the boys never got in trouble. Mom had a soft spot for Dan and Joe. Donna was in the bathroom when it was her turn to dry the dishes.

Every Saturday morning we had to finish our chores before we could play. Doing chores was an obligation that helped the family and the farm, so I was told. Joe and Dan played baseball in the driveway while I cleaned the garage and washed the car.

"Lorraine, you're the oldest and have more responsibility," Mom said, as she stood in the driveway.

"You always say that, but they aren't doing their share."

"Don't worry about your brothers. I'll take care of them." Mom never made the boys do anything. Being the oldest wasn't easy, but I was first in line and got things first and all I had to do was ask. There weren't any rules to follow and I didn't have any hand-me-downs.

The summer I turned 10 Dad bought me a chestnut quarter horse and I named her Lady. Dad said she was my reward for being responsible, working for him during the summer and doing my chores around the house. Donna said it was because I was constantly asking Dad to get me a horse, and Dad did admit that the squeaky wheel gets the grease.

"Horses are a lot of work. You have to ride them every day, feed them twice a day and clean out the barn," Dad said.

"I know, Daddy. I will, I will." Lady was one of the best presents Dad ever gave me.

Dad bought the mare from a horse trader in Sacramento and we brought her home in Grandpa's old white horse trailer. Lady was headstrong, spirited and spooked easily. After Dad drove into the barnyard, I put the rope around her neck and backed her out of the trailer as my family watched.

"Lorraine, what are you doing?" Dad said. "Back her straight out."

"I'm trying to, Dad, but I can't control her. She's nervous and she doesn't know where she is."

Lady stepped off the backside of the trailer ramp and ripped the side of her flank open on the tail hitch.

"Dad, she cut herself. Look at all the blood."

"She'll be all right. Put her in the corral and I'll call the vet. She's going to need stitches."

The gash on her flank was six inches long. Eighteen stitches later, I walked Lady into her new barn and brushed her until dark, when Dad said I had to go home and go to bed. I was afraid Lady was going to hate me. I think she did if I count all the times she threw me off.

I rode my horse every day during the summer with a bareback pad. Dad taught me how to put the bridle on her, but Grandpa's Western saddle was so heavy I couldn't get the saddle on by myself. I bathed her in the ditch under the tree fort Mr. Heil built and she stood in the middle of the running water while we kids played in the tree fort, swinging on the rope across the ditch, jumping on and off her back. It was hot and Lady loved being in the cool water. I taught her to come to me by putting oats in my hand and calling her name. None of my cousins wanted to ride Lady; Donna thought horses were stupid and Joe and Dan were not interested in anything to do with horses. I think they were all afraid of her.

"Dad, watch. She'll come when I call. She's smart," I said, as Dad stood by the corral fence.

"You better stop giving her oats and treats. She's getting fat."

"I ride her every day. Maybe I'm feeding her too much alfalfa in the morning and at night."

We cut back on her feed, but she didn't lose any weight. I went on a trail ride with my two friends, Nina and Lucy, who lived down the road and had horses of their own too. Riding with my girlfriends was a heck of a lot more fun than riding by myself.

"Lorraine, what's wrong with Lady?" Nina asked, as we rode side by side.

"I don't know. She's getting fat so I haven't been feeding her as much. I hope she isn't getting sick," I said, trying to think of an excuse for Lady not wanting to gallop.

The next morning, Dad rushed into my room at 6 a.m. "Get dressed. You need to come out to the barn. Hurry up."

"Dad, what is it? Is something wrong with Lady? I rode her hard yesterday and used the whip and she still wouldn't run. I couldn't keep up with Nina and Lucy."

I ran to the barn behind Dad, nervous that something bad had happened. I opened the barn door and on the straw next to Lady was a colt. He was wobbling around on his skinny legs, his coat wet from being licked by his mother.

"I didn't know Lady was going to have a baby!"

"She must have been out in pasture with the other horses before we brought her home. Looks like you got two horses for the price of one."

"Lady, I'm sorry," I said, as I put my arms around her neck. "I could have killed you and your colt. I thought you were getting fat and I put you on a diet. You must think I'm mean and stupid." I looked at her with tears in my eyes, and then I looked at the colt. He was a bay, with brown hair and a black mane and tail. "I'm going to name him Bay Boy," I told Dad. "Isn't he the most beautiful colt you've ever seen?"

I loved having a new baby colt to brush and hug and play with, but taking care of two horses was tons of work. Grandpa Rominger saved me. He fed my horses every morning when he milked the cows. The horse barn was red-stained wood with a V-shaped, silver tin roof and double doors on each end, large enough to drive a grain harvester through. The horse stalls and corral were on one side in the barn and the cow stalls and corral on the other. In the middle of the barn was an open space full of hay, stacked 10 feet high. A four-foot-wide Jackson fork, attached to a carriage that ran the length of the pitched roof with ropes on a pulley, was used to unload the hay into the barn. Grandpa could swing the fork with exact precision into the middle of the hay pile, swallow a clump of hay with the metal forks and drop it directly in the hay trough on either side of the barn. Grandpa fed and milked the cows every morning and night and at night I helped. He'd milk and I'd feed. Helping Grandpa was my favorite chore.

"Grandpa, can I milk the cow?" I asked, as I bent down beside him.

"Come here. I'll show you how. It takes practice."

Milking the cow was much harder than Grandpa made it look. I had to grab the udder just right, squeeze just right, and pull just right to get the milk to spray in the bucket.

"You develop a rhythm as you go. You have to squeeze and pull at the same time and grab the udder at the top, start to pull down and squ-e-e-z-e."

"I'm afraid I'll hurt her, Grandpa. You better milk the cow. I can't get a drop of milk in the bucket. Besides, the cats are waiting for a drink."

Wild cats lived in the barn and Grandpa liked having them around because they killed the mice and rats. When it was milking time, the cats lined up and waited for a squirt. Grandpa teased me and said he never ever gave them any milk except when I was there, but I knew better. He could squirt the milk in a direct line right into their mouth and not spill a drop.

I was best at feeding the chickens and hunting the eggs.

"Here's the bucket. Remember, don't drop the eggs in the bucket. You have to set them in gently or we won't have any for breakfast," Grandpa said.

Two chicken coops stood next to the cow barn behind Grandpa's house. Fifty chickens lived in the coops and laid dozens of eggs.

"Here chicks, here chicks," I said, throwing the grain on the ground in front of the coops.

I filled up the water pans and feed troughs that were on the dirt in front of the coops.

Dad told me, "Don't forget to put the feed out first. The chickens hear the grain drop in the metal trough and come out of the coop."

The one time I forgot and opened the door to the coop first, it was like a tornado swirling inside. Frightened hens scattered and flew through the air, the straw and dust circling my head getting in my nose and eyes. That was the only time I forgot to feed the chickens first before hunting the eggs. The walls inside the coop were lined from top to bottom with wooden cubbyholes full of straw where the chickens hid to lay their eggs. I never knew what I'd find in each nest. Half the time I stuck my arm in the nest, I got chicken poop all over my hand. That was the bad part about hunting the eggs.

"Grandpa, our eggs are brown. There must be something wrong with them. The eggs in the grocery store are white."

"The eggs are fine. Some people like brown eggs and some people like white eggs. The type of hen determines the color of the egg, so some hens lay white eggs and some hens lay brown eggs."

When Grandpa brought home newborn baby chicks, he put them in the heated incubator tent in the small shed next to the chicken coop. We sat on the floor, stuck our hands inside the tent jammed full of baby chicks, caught one and held it. They were soft and bright yellow and the cutest things ever. Dad was an expert at making chick sounds, so good in fact, that we thought he was holding one in the palm of his hand whenever he made the sound and he teased us all the time. We spent hours playing with the baby chicks, but they didn't stay little and cute for long.

My Dad helped Grandpa feed the chickens and hunt the eggs when he was in grammar school too. During World War II, Grandpa had 150 hens and my Dad was responsible for hunting the eggs, cleaning them and packing them in cartons. Grandpa sold them at the grocery store in Winters, and sometimes Grandma swapped the eggs for groceries. When Dad was 10 he got his first BB gun and loved to shoot the sparrows that ate the chicken feed out of the troughs in the chicken yard.

After Grandpa milked the cow, he brought the milk into the house in a stainless-steel bucket and poured the milk into six-inch-deep, eighteen-inch-wide, round stainless-steel pans. The milk sat overnight on the counter and the cream rose to the top. In the morning, Grandma skimmed off the thick cream to make butter, poured the milk into one-gallon glass jars and cooled it. Raw milk, Grandpa called it, the best milk in the world. It was different than the milk people bought in cartons in the grocery store; that milk was processed. Our milk was pure and straight from the cow.

Dad said the best thing about having our own cows was the thick cream that we used to make cream toast, and you couldn't buy thick, rich cream like that in the grocery store; it had the consistency of mayonnaise. It was best to use plain white bread and we smothered it with the thick cream, then sprinkled sugar all over the top and then sprinkled cinnamon on top of the sugar. The bread went on a cookie sheet in the oven on broil and we let it get nice and golden and crispy on top. We'd wait by the oven door until Mom said it was ready to take out, but we always burnt our mouths because we couldn't wait to let it cool down.

After I helped Grandpa with the chores, it was time to feed my horses, and Dad taught me to clean their feet with a hoof pick. I was afraid my horses would kick me as I stood behind them, putting my weight against a back leg as I picked up a hoof. Dad convinced me they liked getting the manure out of their hooves. Cleaning out the horse barn was harder. I used a pitchfork to pick up the straw covered in manure, loaded it in the wheelbarrow and rolled it out to the manure pile. It stunk, and the stench was so strong it burnt my nostrils and made me sick to my stomach.

"You have to clean out the barn every other day," Dad said. "It's not good for the horses to stand in the manure. It's bad for their hooves."

The poop from two horses piled up quickly. Aunt Joan helped me clean out the barn the day my cousins from Los Angeles came to visit. My cousins were city slickers and had no idea what living on a farm was like. They came to the barn and found me slinging horse poop into the wheelbarrow.

"What are you doing?" Sally asked.

"I'm cleaning out the horse barn."

"Well, I have horses too, but the men who run the stables clean out the stalls. I don't have to do that," my cousin said in disgust, as she turned to go back to the house.

As she did, Aunt Joan said, "The next time anyone is stupid enough to ask you what you're doing, just tell them you're shoveling shit. That'll shut them up." We both laughed, standing in the horse stall in our rubber boots up to our ankles in horse poop.

I joined 4-H and entered Lady in 4-H horse shows. Dad helped me train Lady and haul her around the county to compete. I won a few ribbons, but never placed first. Lady was one hell of a stubborn horse with a mean streak; she had me bluffed and I will admit I was afraid of her. The worst part was, she knew it. I'd jump her over bales of hay and as she galloped up to the bale, she'd stop dead in her tracks and eat the alfalfa. I flew over her head and landed on my butt. You'd think after she did it enough times I'd learn, but no, I was as stubborn as she was. I was determined to show that darn horse I was boss.

"You're strong and smart," Dad said. "Grab those reins and don't be afraid of her. She may be bigger than you, but you're smarter. Use the whip if you have to."

"I don't want to use the whip. I'm afraid she'll buck me off."

In a hurry to meet my friends for a ride after school, I cinched the saddle too tight and when I mounted Lady, she reared up. As I pulled back on the reins, she fell backwards on top of me. The saddle horn knocked me in the ribs and I couldn't breathe. I was so sore I didn't ride for a week.

"Be tough," Dad said. "The only thing to do after a spill is get back up on the horse. Can't let a horse think you're afraid of them."

The next week, I got up the nerve to ride again. After walking Lady through a muddy field, I crossed over the canal on a paved road. The ditch was drying up and hundreds of fish were caught in a small pond in the bottom of the ditch. As the fish flopped and splashed, the noise spooked Lady and she jumped sideways, slipping on her muddy hooves and falling over on the pavement on top of me. One good thing about my horse, she never ran away when I fell off. I couldn't put weight on my leg so I climbed on the bridge rail and threw myself on her. I turned for home and galloped for two miles, using the whip with no thought at all.

"Mom, Mom," I screamed, sitting on Lady at the back door.

"What's wrong? What happened?" Mom asked, as she ran outside with Dad.

"Lady fell over on me crossing the canal on the bridge by the school and I think I broke my leg. I can't put weight on it. You have to help me off."

"How did this happen?" Dad asked.

"She spooks at the dumbest things. Fish were flopping around in the bottom of the ditch and she heard the noise and spooked and slipped and fell over on me."

The doctor cut my pants and boot off. My leg and ankle were broken in several places.

"You have a multiple fracture," the doctor said. "You'll need to wear a cast for several months from your toes to your knee. I'll give you a pair of crutches."

The minute we got home from the doctor, Dad took me out to the barn, put the saddle on Lady and put me on top of her.

"Take the whip," Dad said.

When Dad set his mind to something, I could forget trying to change it. My Dad had a commanding presence and was a strong, authoritative father just like his father had been with him. But my Dad was also a big softy, and he knew when the time called for him to be one or the other. Sometimes I struggled with the tension it caused, but I knew Dad loved me and was doing what he thought best. I was raised to respect my parents and do what I was told, whether I agreed with them or not. Anyway, Dad was right. I was able to ride with my cast on and when I flashed that whip along the side of Lady's head and she caught a glimpse of the whip in the corner of her eye, she straightened right up.

Dad (at left) and Uncle Mick, on butchering day,
circa 1970s

Chapter 6

There wasn't much Dad couldn't do.

He was a laborer, an engineer, a scientist and a businessman. Dad understood weather patterns, soil content and crop yields. Dad's land gave him purpose in life and he was a hard worker from sunup to sundown, which allowed his family and farm to prosper. Dad was opinionated about the state of our country and was a force of conservatism. He had a heart of gold, and was kind and generous with an unwavering faith in God. People in the community liked and respected him. He was a man who lived by his beliefs. As tough as Dad was, he was also gentle.

Dad and I had a ritual. When he taught me to do something new, his instructions were the same—short, sweet and to the point. Whether he was teaching me to play a sport, do a job on the farm or drive his pickup, Dad expected me to get it right the first time. Dad taught me to drive the motorcycle when I was 10. Good thing we rode on dirt.

"Get on and don't touch the tailpipe. It's hot. It'll burn the heck out of you. Pay attention and listen," Dad said, standing next to the motorcycle with his hands on the handlebars. "This is the gas, this is the brake and this is the clutch. You pull in the clutch and click the foot pedal down at the same time and then let out the clutch and give it some gas. Every shift is a click. One click down is first gear, then a click up for second, third and fourth gears. Got it?"

It was as though Dad thought I knew what I was doing and forgot I was a kid. I tried hard to get it right, but it didn't always turn out right the first time.

"What are you doing?" Dad asked, as I sat on the motorcycle, put it in first gear and killed it. "You didn't give it enough gas."

"Dad, you have to show me again. I've never ridden a motorcycle before," I said.

"Watch me and listen."

"I'm afraid it's going to fall over on me and I won't be able to pick it up."

"It won't fall over. Give it some gas. Keep trying."

The motorcycle wasn't as mean and stubborn as my horse and I didn't have to use a whip. Before long, riding the motorcycle was a piece of cake. I never wore a helmet, but Dad forbade me to ride on paved roads, and insisted I wear long sleeves, long pants and boots.

Dad taught all of us kids to ride and we were lucky. We each had a motorcycle and rode every day for years and never had a serious accident. Joe and Dan could do wheelies, and go down into and come up out of the canal, flying 5 feet in the air with one hand on the handlebars and one hand raised in a victory fist, signifying their one-upmanship over their sisters. I was forever getting the motorcycle stuck in the mud, flipped on its side or lying on top of me on a hill, and I didn't have the strength to pick up the darn thing. Nothing was more exhilarating, though, than the four of us racing down the dirt road as fast as we could go, flat-out.

Dad made a go-kart from used equipment parts. The go-kart had a steel frame with wooden planks inside, a steering wheel from a tricycle, wheels from a red wagon and an old lawnmower motor. The road that circled the equipment lot shaped like a football field next to our house was the racetrack.

"Kids, take turns. Share the go-kart, or I'll put it away and none of you will drive. *Capisce?*" Dad asked.

The smile on Dad's face was what I remember as we raced around the lot in his homemade go-kart. Every time the go-kart broke down, he fixed it, lying on the gravel in his long-sleeved, blue cotton work shirt and rolled-up Levis, sweat running down his forehead and neck, his shirt stained dark blue from the sweat. One day, the go-kart went kaput. Between my siblings and Rick, Charlie, Ruth and Bruce racing around the track and driving like bats out of hell, the rubber fell off the wheels, the engine conked out and the steering column bent in two.

We only lived four miles from Winters, but rarely went to town to play with other kids. The eight of us were inseparable with never a shortage of places to play on the farm. Uncle Richard and his family lived on one side of the equipment lot where the shop and the office were located, and we lived on the other.

Grandma and Grandpa had five children and seventeen grandchildren. In addition to my Dad and our family, Uncle Richard, Aunt Evelyne and their kids Rick, Charlie, Ruth and Bruce lived on the farm; Aunt Joan, Uncle Dan and their kids Shannon, Corinne, Barbara, Dan and Yvonne lived in Winters; Aunt Lucille, Uncle Tom and their kids Matt, Diana and Tommy lived in Sacramento, less than an hour away; and Aunt Claire and Romin lived with Grandma and Grandpa.

We all grew up together playing and working on the farm. One of the men who worked for Dad for years, Ron Snodgrass, said we ran around the farm like a bunch of orangutans, hanging in the trees and playing in the tree fort, climbing on the equipment, getting into stuff we shouldn't be messing around with and causing trouble. He called us the Rangity Tango Kids.

"The ditches are almost dry and it's easy to catch fish in the small ponds of water. How many bluegills and catfish do you think we can find in the ditch?" Rick asked.

"We caught bluegills yesterday. Let's ride our bikes to the yellow house and hunt for coyotes," Joe said.

The yellow house was our nickname for the yellow barn in the rolling hills where Uncle Todd sheared sheep in the spring. The sheepherder and his family lived in the yellow house part of the year. Coyotes would attack and kill the baby sheep for food and sometimes the babies died out in pasture because they froze to death during the cold of winter. Dad rode around the farm hoping to spot a coyote and shoot it. He'd throw the dead coyote over the fence and let it hang until it rotted or the turkey buzzards ate it. Dad said it kept other coyotes away, but I'm not sure that was true.

Grandma's restaurant-sized freezer on her back porch was stocked full of Popsicles during the hot summer months. Most afternoons, we lined up at her kitchen door, knowing Grandma bought the Popsicles as a treat for us in the heat of the day. We saved the Popsicle sticks and made barns, forts and corrals held together with Elmer's Glue.

Grandma's basement was our hideaway. We were experts at making pies of flour and water, and when the pies dried hard like rocks, we used a hammer to break them in pieces to get them out of Grandma's aluminum baking tins. The narrow stairs in the kitchen led down to her basement, full of glass canning jars that we filled with things from the farm: dried bugs, snails and butterflies; feathers, seeds and pods; all the right ingredients for a witch's brew. When it was time for Grandma to do her canning, I got stuck hauling the jars up to the kitchen and washing them with boiling water.

"You kids are not supposed to play with my canning jars. How many times have I told you to leave them on the shelves?" Grandma scolded.

"But Grandma, the boys bring creepy things down to the basement and I'm not the only one who hides treasures in the jars," I said.

"You're the oldest and are supposed to know better, so you can help me wash them," Grandma said.

I didn't care. I liked helping Grandma and she taught me to can. Farmers in the area brought Grandma fruits and vegetables from their fields and Grandpa shared his harvest with them. Grandma made the best fruit pies; the secret to her pies and Mom's pies too, she said, was the flaky crust made from lard, otherwise known as pig fat. Grandma knew how to preserve just about everything and Dad said it was because during the Depression when no one had money, farm families did all their own work and made their own supplies. If they didn't grow it or make it, they went without. Grandpa Rominger didn't lose money during the Great Depression; in fact he made money, Dad told me, because he never bought a thing. I thought about the smarts and skills needed to survive when you couldn't buy a thing and had to make do with what you had. Grandma even made their sweet treats from horehound weeds. She'd boil the leaves and make cough drop–size hard candies from the extract. Dad said it tasted like leaves, but it was better than nothing. Grandma was full of stories as I worked alongside her in the kitchen.

"Your father and his brother got in trouble when they were boys for making a mess in the basement. The lard was in cans on the shelves and they poured the lard over the cement floor until it was slippery like an ice-skating rink and slid around the floor in their boots yipping and hollering without a care in the world," Grandma said.

"That must have made a big mess," I said.

"You've never seen such a mess. I thought your Grandfather was going to kill those boys. There was grease everywhere and it took them days to clean the floor with boiling hot water."

"Dad never told me that story."

"I'm not surprised. Your Dad was a tease and a little rascal. I won't forget the day he was swatting your Aunt Claire with a wet dishtowel. When I tried to grab the towel, he wrapped it around her neck and twisted it so tight she passed out."

"My Dad did that?"

"It scared me to death. But your Aunt Claire insisted on playing with her older brothers and ignored her younger sisters. That is, until the day she played cowboys with Rich and Don. They made Claire be the canteen girl, like the girls in the old dance halls, and your dad was yelling, 'Dance, sister, dance.' When she wouldn't dance, he shot at her feet with his BB gun."

"That's funny, Grandma," as I laughed. I could picture my Dad shooting his gun at his sister's feet. Dad was always playing pranks on us too.

"It may be funny now, but it wasn't then," Grandma said. "Your Dad loved to tease Claire. One night we all sat down for dinner and Claire didn't come to the table. I looked at the boys and asked your Dad, 'Where's Claire? Have you done something to her?'"

"'Don't look at me, Mom,' your Dad says. 'I don't know where she is.'"

"'Claire, Claire,' I cried out from the table. 'Dinner is ready.' To make a long story short, I had to walk through the house calling out for her and heard her kicking the door in the upstairs hall closet. Your Dad had tied her up and locked her in the closet and told her if she squealed on him, he'd never play with her again or let her shoot his gun.

"Oh, I remember the winter it rained for weeks and your Dad's boots were always soaked. He asked me to waterproof his boots so I melted lamb fat and smeared the fat on his boots; that's how we waterproofed things in those days. Only I didn't tell him that lamb fat smells much worse than pig fat. He thought it was pretty cool, until he came home from school and said he'd stunk so bad no one would sit by him."

Every year in December, Dad and Grandpa bought nine pigs and fattened them up for a couple of weeks. The week before Christmas, Uncle Todd and Uncle Mick, Grandpa's brothers and their families, along with Dad's brother and three sisters and their families, came to Grandma and Grandpa's house to butcher pigs. It took two days, and the first day was the worst. That was the day they killed the pigs, and I watched the men do it once. I never went out to the barn on the first day of butchering again.

"Sweetie, why are you crying?" Mom asked, as I ran into Grandma's kitchen.

"Grandpa shot the pig between the eyes and Mr. Heil slit its throat and drained the blood into a pan."

"I told you not to go near the barn. Stay in the house with us."

"I stood outside the shed and peeked through a hole in the siding. I feel sorry for those pigs."

"You know your father buys pigs to kill so we have pork to eat during the year."

"I'm not ever going to eat pig again."

After the pigs were dead, they were gutted and lowered into a huge, metal tub resting over a fire pit full of boiling water that scorched the hair off their bodies. Grandpa built a large wooden rack by the barn next to his house where he hung the pigs, cut off the heads and feet, and left the bodies to dry overnight. The women stayed in the kitchen cooking breakfast and lunch for the men and I knew why they never went outside the first day. There were lots of people to feed with nine families butchering and each family took home the pork from one pig. All of us sat at the 30-foot table in Grandma and Grandpa's dining room, the same table where we would sit in a few days for breakfast and supper on Christmas.

"Dad, what do you do with the pigs' blood?" I asked, as he stood at the sink on the back porch washing his hands covered in dry blood.

"Mr. Heil keeps it for his family and friends and they make blood sausage."

"Yuck, that's disgusting."

"You don't have to eat it. Some people like blood sausage. Everything in life has a purpose." Things were always black and white with my Dad; there wasn't much gray in-between.

The second day the men cut the pigs into sections and laid the pork on long wooden tables set up in Grandma's garage.

The women wrapped the meat with white butcher paper and butcher tape like at the meat shop in town and I helped. Once the pig was dead, it didn't bother me as much, and Mom taught me to wrap meat like the butcher. We wrote on the package in black felt pen the date and description of the cut: pork chops, pork roast, pork ribs, pork loin. Then we made fresh link sausage. One of us fed the pork scraps into the meat grinder while one of us turned the crank and one of us slid the casing onto the nozzle at the bottom of the grinder. The casing filled with ground-up pork and reminded me of a long, fat hot dog. We coiled the links on the tabletop and when a hole appeared in the casing, we'd tie off the casing and start over. We spent hours the first day scraping the casings for the link sausage, which were nothing more than the pig's intestines that we soaked all night so they were good and clean. Then we hung the three-to-four-foot links on wooden slats tied with string in the smokehouse until Christmas morning.

Once the pig was cut into sections, the skin and fat were cut from the meat. The skin was tough and white, and there was an inch of fat between the pig's skin and the meat. I helped cut the fat into one-inch squares that were boiled over a blazing fire in a huge metal vat lined with a metal basket to collect the cracklings and a press on the top that separated the liquid. We saved coffee cans all year to pour the clear liquid fat into, and once it hardened it turned white again. The lard was the secret to Mom's pie crust.

Pie Crust

1-1/4 cups lard
3 cups flour
1 egg
1 tsp salt
1 tbsp vinegar
5 tbsp water

Mix together the flour and lard with a pie blender. Beat the egg, salt, water and vinegar together and add the liquid mixture to the flour and lard. Blend together. Sprinkle lots of flour on the crust and pastry board before flattening the crust with a rolling pin.

Bake at 450 for 12 minutes if cooking the crust before adding the filling.

Butchering the chickens didn't require as many people, so Dad and Grandpa did most of the work. The morning I was in Grandpa's back yard, saw him hold the chicken's neck over a tree stump and whack it off with an axe, I knew I wasn't helping butcher the chickens. The chicken flopped around the yard for seconds without a head before it collapsed. That was enough for me.

"Come here and help me burn the feathers off these chickens," Dad said. "I'll show you how easy it is."

"Dad, I feed the chickens and hunt the eggs. I'm not going to help you kill them."

He let me off the hook.

When Donna and I came home carrying boxes full of wrapped chickens, Mom stared at us and said, "Look at you girls. You're filthy. You have blood and chicken feathers all over your clothes. It's time you experience something other than butchering and farm work. I think you need some culture in your life."

"What do you mean, Mom?" Donna asked.

"We've talked about this. You both said you wanted to learn to play a musical instrument, and Momo Cody agreed to give you girls her piano. She doesn't use it so I had it delivered this morning. Go look, it's in the living room."

"But we don't know how to play the piano," I said.

"I signed you up for piano lessons with Mrs. Stephanie."

Mrs. Stephanie was the organist at our church and lived down the road a couple of miles. We were excited to take lessons until Mom informed us we had to practice every day after school for an hour.

"An hour?" we both asked at the same time in disbelief.

"You girls have to practice or it won't do any good to take lessons." Mom gave in. An hour turned into thirty minutes.

"You girls are impossible," Mom said. "I thought this was something you wanted to do."

"It's something you wanted us to do, Mom," Donna said.

It was a fight every day after school, and even though we took lessons for a couple of years, Mom got tired of arguing with us. So much for culture.

Mom did lots of special things for us kids, especially on our birthdays. Birthdays were about family, a birthday dinner and a birthday cake with candles and lots of presents. Mom never missed our birthdays and she always invited our aunts, uncles and first cousins; it was a full house. We played cards and checkers, hopscotch and hide-and-seek, and Uncle Richard walked around stalking everyone taking pictures, telling us to look at him and smile. Drove us crazy, but we did love looking at the photos after he had them developed and brought them to the next family party.

Dad had a game named The Labyrinth, a wooden box the size of a man's boot box with a maze painted on the movable top. The point of the game was to get the little metal ball from the beginning of the maze that started in one corner of the top to the end of the maze in the opposite corner, following the single path. The challenge was that the top of the box moved back and forth and tiny little holes were cut next to the path, just big enough for the little ball to drop into. The movement was controlled by knobs on the side of the box that you had to turn just ever so slightly and in unison to keep the top level and the little ball from dropping into one of many holes. Dad practiced for hours and he was the only one of us who could get that little metal ball from one end of the maze to the other. We kids tried and tried. We'd sit around in a big circle in the den, one of us in the center with the box, staring intently at the maze, watching the little ball, guiding it, turning the knobs slowly and carefully, until a big "OHHH" sounded from the room and everyone knew the ball had dropped. Most of the time we played Horses, our favorite game of tag. Rick and I were the fastest runners, so we never got to be on the same team.

"What kind of birthday cake do you want?" Mom would ask. "My favorite. Same as Dad's," I always said.

Mom's Star Lite Double Delight was the best chocolate cake, homemade from scratch.

The chocolate cake was even better when it was smothered with her home-made vanilla ice-cream. It was the creamiest, sweetest ice-cream we had ever tasted, much better than store-bought ice-cream. Mom said it tasted so good because of the thick cream she used that Grandpa skimmed off the raw milk. When I was a little kid, it took Dad hours to make the ice-cream because we didn't have an automatic ice-cream maker and he had to whip the ice-cream with a hand crank. Dad was stubborn about doing it his way, but he gave in and Mom bought an automatic ice-cream maker. It seemed ridiculous to sit on the back porch for an hour turning the crank. Once we got the machine, all we had to do was attach the motor to the two-gallon steel container Mom filled with the creamy mixture, put the container in the metal tub, cover it with ice and lots of rock salt to keep the ice from melting, and turn on the motor. In no time at all, we had thick vanilla ice-cream.

Mom won first place at the county fair in the cake competition. Whenever we went to a friend's house for dinner, Mom was asked to bring dessert. She was known for her baked goods: apricot cookies, coconut-cream pie and lemon-meringue pie. Dad said there wasn't a better cook or baker in town. Mom never had a job away from home, away from us kids, and could always be found in the kitchen. We were all expected to pitch in whenever Mom needed help.

"How come we don't get an allowance?" I asked once. "All the other kids in my class get an allowance when they do chores."

"An allowance? You live here, don't you?" Mom asked. "Joe and Dan live here too and you never make them do anything," I said.

"They're little boys. You're the oldest and I count on you to set a good example."

"You always say that, Mom."

Star Lite Double Delight

(2) 3-oz packages cream cheese
1/2 cup butter
1 tsp vanilla
6 cups powdered sugar

1/4 cup warm water
4 squares bittersweet chocolate
1/2 cup shortening (margarine or lard)
2-1/4 cups cake flour
1-1/2 tsp baking soda
1 tsp salt
3 eggs
3/4 cup milk

Cream together first 3 ingredients. Sift the powdered sugar and put 3 cups into the creamed mixture and stir. Add the remaining 3 cups sugar and the warm water and stir. Melt the chocolate in a double boiler and blend in. Take out 2 cups for the frosting. Add shortening and stir. Add eggs and stir. Sift together flour (best to use cake flour and not regular baking flour), baking soda and salt. Add milk and flour to mixture, ending with flour. Put in two 9" greased baking pans and bake for 25–30 minutes. Take cake out before it is completely done as it will cook in the hot pans. Let cool. Turn pans over on cooking racks and remove cake from pans. Use a knife to cut around the pan's edges to loosen the cake if necessary.

Buffalo Bill Cody at a Wild West Show, circa 1905

Chapter 7

WHS

A picture of "Buffalo Bill" Cody hung on the living room wall in our house.

Dressed in a fancy, suede, cream-colored cowboy outfit with fringe on the shirt and a white cowboy hat, Buffalo Bill sat tall on a Palomino holding a rifle. Mom's last name was Cody before she married Dad, and I wanted to know how we ended up on a farm four miles north of Winters with Buffalo Bill watching over us.

"I moved here when I was a baby," Dad said. "Your Grandpa Rominger bought 3,000 acres with his brother Todd, and they moved their families here in the early 1930s. Your Great-Grandpa Charles was Grandpa Rominger's father and came to America from Bitz, Germany, in 1870 with his parents. I think he was 9 at the time. After docking in New York, they traveled on the railroad to Sacramento and moved to Yolo County. Your Great-Grandpa Charles married Elizabeth Blickley and they had 11 children. One of them was your Grandpa Albert."

As I sat next to Dad on the couch, he turned the pages in the photo album full of pictures. "How did Grandpa meet Grandma? Is that them?" I asked, as I pointed to a photo.

"Yes, that's your grandparents on the day they got married. Your Grandpa met your Grandma when she came to Yolo County to teach in a one-room schoolhouse. Grandma was born in a small town in Washington. Her father, George Erhardt, was born in New York in the early 1870s after his German-born parents immigrated to the United States. That's a picture of your Grandma and her parents," Dad said, pointing to another photo. "When your Grandma's Dad moved west, he first worked in Alaska during the gold rush and married Mary Keating, whose parents came from

Ireland on a boat around Cape Horn. Your Grandma was one of five children, and when she grew up she came to California to attend Teacher's College in Sacramento. When your Grandma accepted a position at Clover School in Yolo County she was engaged to another man, but that didn't last long. According to Grandma, your Grandpa was good-looking and very persuasive. They got married in 1924 and I was born five years later, after your Uncle Richard."

"Dad, I know Mom wasn't born here. She didn't come from a farm family. She doesn't even know how to ride a horse. Mom can't be related to Buffalo Bill," I said, as I pointed to his picture on the wall.

"Your Mom moved to Winters in 1943 when she was 13. She was born in Westwood, a small lumber town in the mountains of northern California. Red River Lumber Company built the town for their employees who worked in the lumber mill and her father Charles, your Popo Cody, was a milkman and delivered milk in glass bottles that he left on people's doorsteps."

"Popo's last name is Cody. Did he know Buffalo Bill?"

"You better let your Mom tell you about her side of the family. She knows a lot more about those hoodlums than I do."

"Hoodlums? Don, don't say things like that," Mom said, as she walked into the room. "Your father doesn't mean that." She looked at Dad and let out a sigh. "He's just teasing you." Mom sat down on the couch and turned to the next page in the album.

"Your Popo Cody never met Buffalo Bill, but they are related and descendants of the American ancestors of the Cody family who settled in Massachusetts in the late 1600s. Buffalo Bill lived in the Midwest and died in 1917 and your Popo was born in 1908. Buffalo Bill was a nickname he acquired after the Civil War because he killed thousands of buffalos to supply meat for the workers building the cross-country railroad. He became famous for his Wild West shows, where he would ride on his white horse and shoot things out of the air with Annie Oakley. His first name was William, the same name as Popo's father. Your Great-Grandpa William moved west from Illinois to California and married Carrie McKnight in the early 1900s. They had five boys and one of them was Charles, your Popo Cody and my father. When Popo was a young man he moved to Westwood for work and met Leona Williams, my mother and your Momo Cody, and they married in 1928. I was born two years later."

"Is this a picture of Momo Cody when she was a little girl?" I asked, as I pointed to a photo.

"No, that's her Grandmother, your Great-Great-Grandma, and she came to California from Iowa as a child in the 1850s on a wagon train across the plains. She kept a diary about the trip, and during an Indian attack members of the wagon train were killed, including her father. That's her," Mom said, pointing to her picture.

"She doesn't have any shoes on and her dress is torn and dirty. They were poor, Mom, weren't they?" I asked, as I touched the photo.

"Her name was Luduska and her family settled in California where she married a man named Allen Williams. They had a son, John, and he married Sara Winkel in the late 1890s. John and Sara had nine children and your Momo Cody was their fourth child. You can look at the family album whenever you want. Now you know how you got here and where we came from and why the photo of Buffalo Bill Cody is on the wall. He's your relative."

Popo Cody moved his family to Winters in 1943 to go into business with his brother Bill, who owned a service station and a convenience store located just across the narrow two-lane bridge over Putah Creek outside of town. Bill also owned a resort park with cabins on the creek that people rented during the summer and a bar and hall in town where people threw parties, the same hall where my parents had their wedding reception.

As a child, I was surrounded by twenty-five great-aunts and uncles, visiting them with my grandparents and parents, sitting on their laps, and listening to stories about their childhood. They grew up poor and worked hard to make a better life for their families. The Romingers, Erhardts, Codys and Williamses were large people; no small or short genes ran in my family. Mom and Dad were born into disciplined, hardworking, traditional American families. The men were the providers and went to work every day. If the men didn't work, there was no money. The women were the caretakers who stayed home.

Grandpa Rominger and his brothers and sisters worked the land from the time they were kids. None of them attended high school. They saved every penny and bought farms, or married farmers who lived in Yolo County. According to Dad, people thought there was something different about the Romingers. They stuck together and helped each other through thick and thin—men of the soil with a deep love for their land. Grandpa had six brothers and they worked on each other's farms to keep their labor costs to a minimum. The running joke around our house was that Dad had dirt in his veins, not blood. Farming was not just a job; it was a way of life.

When Dad was a kid he worked on the farm, as his father and grandfather before him, alongside horses and mules.

They didn't have much motorized equipment back then and Dad's favorite mules were Maude and Hazel. Farm laborers occupied the small bunkhouse during planting and harvesting and Grandma cooked meals as part of their wages. Breakfast was at 5:30 a.m. and they worked till sundown and the work was hard and physical.

"Mom, do you remember your first date with Dad?"

"Oh, your Dad. Well, he was the star athlete of his class in high school and was tall and strong. He lettered in track, basketball, boxing and football and had the biggest hands and feet I had ever seen. In fact when your Dad was a senior, he was undefeated in the high jump and the high hurdles, and the football and basketball teams won the league championships and your Dad was the star on both teams. All the guys on the teams gave him such a bad time and he said his big hands and feet helped him excel in sports. Not sure I believed that. Anyway, there were 140 kids at Winters High School and without a doubt, your Dad was a force to be reckoned with. No one messed with Big Bad Don. Oh, and your Dad was also student body president his senior year. But off the field, he was shy and bashful and every girl in high school had a crush on handsome Don Rominger," Mom explained, with a smile on her face.

Dad interrupted, "Your Mom was the new girl in town, good-looking, outgoing, and boy, did she know how to dress. It wasn't long before every boy wanted a date with your Mom. I'd say the girls in high school were jealous of her and that's why they nicknamed her Squirrely Cooty, a nickname she hated, but she was skinny and had bird legs so there wasn't much to argue about."

"Don, that's not true. Don't tell her that."

"Everyone called you Squirrely Cooty."

"That's not what's important about the night we met; get on with your side of the story or I'm finishing it."

"When your Mom was a junior in high school, she was elected cheerleader and I was a senior and the running back on the football team. No one could touch me," Dad said, as he leaned toward me and smiled. "It was Homecoming and your Mom didn't have a date for the dance."

"I'll tell the story," Mom said, winking at Dad. "Your Dad won't tell it like it happened. I didn't have a date for the dance and I was a cheerleader and yes, it was embarrassing. But if I'd waited for your Dad to ask me out, it never would have happened, so I took things into my own hands. I remember exactly what I said to the girls at the game that night. 'I'll bet you a dollar I can get a date with Don for the dance tonight.'

"'Come on Shirley, how in the world are you going to manage that?'" the girls asked.

"'You just wait. I'll be at the dance with Don,' I said to them.

"As soon as the game ended, I walked off the football field to the parking lot behind the gym where the guys on the team parked their cars. I spotted your Dad's car and walked up to it, grabbed the passenger-side door handle, got in the front seat, closed the door and waited. It seemed like hours went by. I kept looking behind me towards the locker room and the door finally opened and your Dad came out."

"Were you scared? Did you think Dad was going to get mad at you for sitting in his car?"

"I don't remember what I was thinking. As he walked to his car, he bent down, noticing someone in the front seat and stared at the car as he walked, not sure what was going on. As he got closer, my heart was racing and I didn't know what I was going to say. Your Dad opened the door, sat down and looked at me.

"'I wanted to tell you what a great game you played. You won the game for us tonight,' I said to him."

I looked at Dad as Mom told the story and he rolled his eyes and shook his head.

"Your Dad didn't say a word. *Why doesn't he say something?* I thought to myself. I remember looking at him and saying, 'I thought maybe you'd like to buy me a Coke to celebrate.'

"There was a long pause. 'Oh...well sure, I guess,' your Dad said, a bit taken by surprise. I knew I'd won my bet.

"You should have seen the look on the girls' faces," Mom said, as she retold the story.

"'How did you get Don to bring you to the dance? What did you do?' my girlfriends asked, when your Dad and I walked into the gym.

"'Where's my dollar?' I said to the girls. 'Don't keep asking me what happened because I'm not going to tell you. Let's just say he couldn't resist.'"

Mom said she didn't tell her girlfriends how she got the date with Dad, but she told us the story over and over. Dad said that wasn't exactly how it happened.

Mom and Dad had a date or two with other people, but Dad said, "I never wanted to go out with anyone other than your Mom. No one was as much fun as she was, or as nice, or as pretty."

Dad graduated from high school with thirty-six seniors and attended the University of California at Davis. He enrolled in a two-year course in agriculture and played varsity football, boxed, ran track and lettered in all sports. He graduated with a degree in agriculture and talked his dad into buying their first bag of fertilizer when he came home. Dad and Uncle Richard also talked Grandpa into leveling the fields so they could irrigate and plant row crops instead of only growing barley and wheat. It was what farmers were starting to do, Dad told Grandpa. They also leased land from other farmers so they could expand their operation and grow a variety of crops including alfalfa, milo, sunflowers and sugar beets. Mom worked as a secretary for a local trucking company and attended junior college for two years. When Dad graduated from Davis and came back to the farm to work, they got married in 1950.

Dad after a deer hunt, circa 1970s

Chapter 8

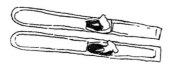

There was never a dull moment around our house.

When Donna was six, Mom bought her a brown suede Indian skirt with fringe on the bottom that she didn't take off for two years. Donna wore it everywhere, much to Mom's objection. Every time we left the house, Donna ran to our bedroom and put on her Indian skirt.

"Donna, you can't wear that Indian skirt to the party. Why don't you wear your new dress?" Mom asked.

"I'm wearing this. You can't make me put on that stupid dress," Donna said.

"You get back in your room and put on your dress."

Donna marched to her room, closed the door and sat on the bed. We waited and Dad sat in the car in the driveway honking the horn.

"You kids get in the car with your father," Mom said.

Donna didn't care. She'd sit in her room for hours. I swear she thought she was Pocahontas. We waited in the car while Dad took bets.

"Donna or Mom?" he asked.

"Donna," we said.

Dad got fed up and took off and drove around the farm for a few minutes, trying to make Donna think we'd left her and Mom behind, but it didn't work. Donna outlasted Mom every time. In the beginning it was funny, but as time went by it got on all our nerves.

Joe was Johnny Ringo, the fastest gun in the West, quicker than all the rest. He dressed in a cowboy shirt and jeans with dark tan suede chaps, a cowboy hat and boots and a belt with a pistol in each side holster. He looked like a miniature John Wayne and walked around the house shooting all of us, twirling his pistols, blowing on the ends of the barrels every time he fired the caps.

Dan wanted to be a football player for the Los Angeles Rams. He wore a Rams jersey and helmet and carried his football under his arm, spending hours in the yard punting the ball, practicing for the day the recruiters would show up. Dan plastered his and Joe's bedroom door with L.A. Rams stickers, and stickers about farming. "Farmers do it in the Dirt," "Eat American Lamb, 16-million Coyotes Can't Be Wrong." The door hasn't changed.

I dressed up in Dad's cowboy boots and hat and sometimes in Mom's high heels. In my favorite picture, I'm 2, posing in my diaper, standing in Dad's cowboy boots that swallow my legs with his cowboy hat resting on the back of my head. Mom had a collection of heels and purses, hats and gloves. Her style was classic and simple and glamorous. In a photo that was taken of her standing in the newly furnished dining room of our house in 1959 for an article in the paper, her shoulder-length dark hair curls softly around her face and she is wearing a short-sleeve, floral-print dress with a tight-belted waist and full skirt. She'd had three of us kids by then and I bet her waist wasn't more than 20 inches. Mom was always skinny. The feature story, "Yolo County Living," ran in the *Sacramento Bee* with photos of Mom and us kids in our house and Dad out in the field on the harvester. It was a story about our family's farming enterprise: my Dad, his brother and father farming together growing irrigated row crops and grain.

My Dad was handsome with a full head of hair and he usually wore a casual white shirt or T-shirt, Levis and cowboy boots with a dark pilot's jacket. Dad was 6'3", Mom was 5'7": both dark-haired, good-looking, the perfect couple. Dad was tan from working on the farm and Mom was fair-skinned with lots of freckles. It was her Irish heritage. I got my freckles from Mom and we laughed that we both had freckles on our bums.

Most of the time we kids ran around the farm barefoot in cut-offs and T-shirts. The first half of summer we lived in our swimsuits. From the time we started first grade until we graduated from high school, we swam on the city swim team every summer, all of us except Dan. The first day Dan went to practice he couldn't swim the length of the 25-yard pool. Mrs. Becker was the assistant coach and she was big and mean.

"Dan, let go of the side of the pool," Mrs. Becker yelled, as she stepped on Dan's fingers.

"I can't make it," he gulped, as his head went underwater.

"Stop being mean to my brother. I'm going to tell my Mom," I said. It was my job to protect my little brother.

"Dan, swim to the end of the pool. Don't stop. Keep swimming," Mrs. Becker said.

Every time Dan grabbed the edge of the pool, she stepped on his fingers. Dan went home and didn't come back. He told Mom he was going to drown.

Dan was the youngest of the eight of us kids who lived on the farm and had a hard time keeping up. He was the baby and, I must confess, we teased him and ran off without him; Joe and my cousins picked on him. It's not a wonder that Dan felt left out and didn't want to play with us. School was difficult for him too, according to Mom.

"Shirley, Dan is not doing well in class. He can't read and he can't do math. I'm afraid he's not very smart," his teacher said, in a meeting with Mom.

"How dare you say that to me! How dare you say that about my son! You're his teacher and you're supposed to help him and encourage him, for crying out loud. Do you know what I think, I think you aren't very smart," Mom said.

Mom noticed Dan's eye wandered and appeared stuck on the outside of his eye socket and she took him to see an eye specialist.

"Dan has a lazy eye and needs to wear corrective glasses," the doctor said. "I'm sure once his eyes adjust to the lens, he'll be fine."

Mom marched back into school and told that teacher a thing or two. Mom removed Dan from her class and made sure he never had that teacher again. Dan wore corrective glasses with a red line in the center of the lens and it wasn't long before his eyes improved and he was doing better in school.

Mom may have been a stay-at-home mom, but she had a mind of her own and when it came to her family, you had better not cross her. She was as tough as she needed to be.

When I look back on Dan being the youngest in a group of highly competitive, rough farm kids, I'm sure it wasn't a picnic, but it didn't bother Dan if he wasn't the best at everything he tried to do. Joe, on the other hand, was smart, a great athlete and excelled at everything. He had to be perfect, just like Dad, and nothing less was good enough. Joe and Dan fought like cats and dogs and drove Mom nuts. She said they were going to end up killing one another.

"Joe, Dan. Stop fighting," Mom said. "Dan, stop teasing your brother. You're asking for it. You're going to get hurt."

One day she tried to stop the boys by chasing them down the hall with her girdle in her hand. The metal clips on the straps that held up her stockings clinked against each other.

"Dan, look out for Mom. Here comes the beater," Joe said.

The boys nicknamed Mom "the beater" and called her that for years. We all laughed, but it annoyed Mom to no end, because she never touched them with the girdle. They outran her every time.

Sometimes their fights got serious, like the day Dan chased Joe down the hall with a kitchen knife and Joe ran in the bathroom and locked the door.

"Come out, you big baby," Dan yelled, standing in front of the bathroom door with the knife.

"You're crazy, I'm not coming out," Joe hollered.

"Then I'll come in and get you," Dan said, as he started slashing the door with the knife.

Joe got so scared he jumped out the bathroom window and ran to the shop to get Dad.

Sometimes Mom went to the grocery store and left me in charge. It was fine when the boys were small because I was bigger and stronger and the boys were afraid of me and did what I said. But as they got older and bigger and I got in the middle of their fights, it was a losing battle. It wasn't long before I had no control over them and they'd laugh and run away from me.

I was no angel; I beat up my sister. Donna grew up tough to protect herself from me and talked back to everyone, including Mom. We were both tomboys—raised on the farm, driving tractors, playing sports, competing with the boys. Growing up, Dad took us hunting and fishing, which I hated, and I cried every time an animal was hurt or killed. Donna called me a crybaby; she didn't cry about anything.

"Donna, I told you not to call your sister names," Mom said.

"I'll do whatever I want. You can't make me do what I don't want to do. You are not my boss."

"Really? Well, let's see what your father has to say about that."

"Don, I don't know what I'm going to do with that child. She's impossible, she won't do her homework or pick up her room, and she took a cigarette out of your jacket and I caught her out in the field smoking."

"Where is she now?" Dad said.

"She's in her room sick to her stomach."

"Good, let her stay in her room and be sick. I'll talk to her in the morning."

But Dad never talked to us about that kind of stuff, he let Mom be the bad guy. Dad let us do crazy things and Mom was the one to clean up the mess. Mom had just turned 20 when she and Dad got married. By the time Mom was 29 she had four kids, and I know the strain of having four kids and no help got to her every now and then. We drove her nuts and so did Dad, on occasion, like the nights we went to the drive-in movies. It was cheap family entertainment and Mom loved movies. Dad did too. John Wayne was his favorite action hero.

"Dad, I can't see. The back seat is too crowded and the boys won't sit still," I said.

"Why don't you and your sister get up on the roof of the car?"

"Don, that's not a good idea letting the kids lay on top of the car," Mom said.

"We'll be careful," I said.

"Don, you need to help the girls get up on the roof. What if they fall off and hurt themselves?"

"Take off your shoes. I don't want you to scratch the top of my car," Dad said, as he laid blankets on top and helped us up.

"Dad, how come the girls get to lie on the top of the car? I want to get up there," Joe said.

"Me too," Dan said.

"Girls, you go up for the first movie and then the boys get a turn," Dad said.

"Dad, that's not fair. You always let the girls do things first," Joe said.

Mom got irritated with Dad for starting the whole game and went to the snack bar to get sodas and popcorn. It never failed; one of us would slip and fall off the car or roll off the top of the car when the pillow fight started.

"Don, I don't know why you have to start things like this with the kids. It turns into a fight or someone gets hurt," Mom said, when she returned.

"Dad, I want to get back in the car," I said.

"What's wrong with you?" Dad said, as I opened the car door in my pajamas wrapped in a blanket.

"They shot all the horses and the sheep," I replied.

"They shot all the cowboys too," Dad pointed out.

"I don't care about those cowboys. They're bad guys."

"The horse was hurt. They had to shoot it."

"When my horse got hurt we didn't shoot her."

"Sonoma beach." (That was Dad's slang for son-of-a-bitch, which he thought we didn't know, but we did.)

"Don," Mom said.

"If it's not one thing, it's another. These kids are never happy."

"Don't blame the kids," Mom said.

Dad liked to roam around the range in his pickup, just like John Wayne riding across the plains on his horse. John Wayne killed bad cowboys, Dad killed wild game. Dad liked nothing more than to brag about how big the deer was or how many points the antlers had. The Romingers and Codys were known for their hunting and fishing stories. Between Grandpa Rominger's ten brothers and sisters and Popo Cody's four brothers, there wasn't an animal they hadn't seen or shot.

Popo Cody loved to hunt and fish, but Momo Cody was the deadeye. After Popo sold his business and retired, they bought an Airstream trailer and spent part of the year at Mt. Lassen and on the Klamath River in Northern California. Dad, Joe and Dan drove north to hunt and fish with Popo and Momo. When the boys got home, stories flew around the kitchen table, and if it hadn't been for the Polaroid photos that Momo took, I'm not sure Mom, Donna and I would have believed them. Photos were hard to dispute.

Fishing was one thing. They stayed in the trailer at night and fished on the river during the day. Hunting was a bigger deal, with them camping in the freezing cold and sleeping in tents in the woods. Joe was best at telling stories when they got home.

"It must be below freezing," I said to Momo. "I can't sleep."

"So Momo says, 'Wrap the sleeping bag around you. Come here and sit by the fire with me and I'll warm some large rocks and put them in your sleeping bag. It's a little trick I learned.'

"Momo got the rocks as hot as she could and wrapped them in newspaper. She put the rocks in Dan's and my sleeping bags and our bags got warm, fast. I pulled the bag over my head and started to fall asleep, but after a few minutes I couldn't breathe and started to choke. My sleeping bag filled with smoke and as I pulled my head out of the bag I saw Dan's sleeping bag was smoking too. I jumped out coughing and yelling and Momo came running out of her tent screaming, 'Get out of your bags. They're on fire!' Dan rolled out of his bag coughing and gasping. Momo grabbed the bucket full of water, dumped the rocks out of the bags and doused the rocks with water. The newspaper was smoking. Our bags smelled like smoke so bad I'm not sure what was worse, the cold or the smell. Dad and Popo never let her hear the end of it. I thought Dan was going to die from smoke inhalation."

Mom, Donna and I went hunting with them once. Everyone got up early in the morning to hunt and the three of us stayed in camp. Mom brought a transistor radio and Donna and I were singing songs and dancing around the campfire. Dad always brought more than one rifle on the hunt and he'd left one on the picnic table.

"Mom, be quiet. Don't say anything. Donna, don't turn around fast. There's a deer behind you," I said.

There in front of me was a forked horn walking through camp. We froze and watched the buck less than 20 feet away. On the table sat Dad's deer rifle.

"Your Dad is not going to believe this," Mom whispered.

"Wait until he gets back and we tell him what happened." When Dad, the boys and Momo and Popo came back to the campground for lunch, I said, "Dad, did you get a deer?"

"Didn't see a one," he said, shaking his head.

"We did."

"What do you mean?"

"A big buck walked through camp not far from the table. We were sitting right here."

"You mean to tell me a buck walked into camp and you just sat there?" Dad asked, looking at Mom.

"What did you want me to do? Shoot the deer in camp in front of the girls? Every person in the campground would think I was shooting my daughters. Anyway, I don't know how to shoot that rifle."

"Well, I'll be damned," Popo said. "We haven't seen a deer since we got here and one walks through camp and you let him get away."

"I had no intention of killing that deer."

We told the story to everyone when we got home, but Dad didn't see the humor in it.

Dad also went hunting with his favorite hunting partner, Warren. Warren was a crazy mountain man who went days without taking a shower whether he was hunting or not. He knew lots of people in California who owned land where he and Dad hunted.

"Don and I walked for hours and saw a couple of bucks," Warren told us. "They were too far away and we didn't have a shot. We tracked them through tall shrubs and heard something move in the brush in front of us and stopped to pinpoint the noise. I motioned to your Dad to circle the brush and flush out the deer. As I started to walk the other way all of a sudden I heard a crashing sound, sticks popping and shrub limbs breaking when a 100-pound wild boar charged out of the brush headed straight to Don. That boar was 30 feet away when he charged. 'Don,' I shouted, 'Shoot the bastard.' That boar took your Dad by surprise and scared the hell out of him. It happened so damn fast I think Don forgot what he was doing. By the time he aimed his rifle and shot, that damn pig wasn't more than two feet in front of him and I thought Don was going to shoot himself in the foot. The rifle backfired so hard your Dad fell flat on his ass. Thank God he killed that damn pig or its tusk would have been stuck in your Dad's leg. I laughed myself sick seeing your old man on his ass with that wild pig sitting dead at his feet. He'd never admit it, but your Dad didn't know what hit him," Warren laughed.

Dad never lived that story down. Of course to this day, he won't admit it happened like that.

No calendar on the farm was complete without the beginning of deer, pheasant, dove and duck seasons. The animals didn't have a chance; poor things were dead on opening day. Dad rode around the hills before the season started and knew where the animals were hiding. Even though Dad had "No Trespassing" signs on his land, during hunting season strangers ignored the signs and drove around on his roads like they owned the place. One year it rained like crazy and some kids got stuck in the mud and had the nerve to walk to Dad's door and ask him to pull them out.

"You can see how muddy the roads are," Dad told them. "I suggest you walk home and when things dry out in a few days, come back with your father."

They came back in a couple of days with their father, and Dad pulled their pickup out with the tractor and charged them $300. He said they got off cheap, considering the time it would take him to grade the road to get the ruts out.

Opening Day came once a year and Dad invited his friends to hunt at sunup. If it was bird season, they brought the dead birds to the house to pick the feathers that flew around the yard for days. We ate every bird Dad shot, except the crows. After deer season, we ate venison more than I care to remember, or more than I was told.

"Mom, this is the best beef steak with dumplings you've ever made," I said.

"What are you talking about? That's not beef," as Mom looked at me with a surprised look on her face.

"Well, if it's not beef, then what is it?"

"It's venison."

"You mean it's deer? All these years I've been eating deer and I thought it was beef? I've told you a million times how great the beef is and you never said a word."

"I never said it was beef. We've been eating the deer your Dad shoots since you were old enough to eat meat."

"Why didn't you tell me? I'm never eating venison again."

I saw Dad kill a deer once. The fields surrounding our house were flat, irrigated row-crop ground. Grandpa's farm sat at the foot of the coastal mountains and as we drove through the flat fields toward the mountains, the topography changed to rolling plains planted with barley and wheat, golden grain that swayed in the winds during the summer before harvest, reminding me of a quiet, yellow sea. Driving on, the rolling plains turned to rolling hills, covered with scrub grass and oak trees. This was the range, a haven for does, fawns and bucks.

As Dad and I came around a blind curve, in the road on the crest of the hill in front of us stood a forked horn. Dad slammed on the brakes and pulled his rifle from the gun rack behind me.

"Don't move. Be quiet."

"Dad, please don't shoot the deer," I said, as he fired the rifle. The shot rang against the hills with a vibration.

Dad missed and the buck disappeared over the hill. I was happy, for a second.

"Hold on," Dad said, as he stepped on the gas and raced up the hill.

At the top of the hill was a blood trail that led through the yellow grass and down to a clump of oak trees in a ravine. "Stay here."

I knew there was nothing I could say. It wasn't more than a few minutes before I heard another shot. Dad walked out of the trees and toward the pickup, got in and sat down. I had tears in my eyes and stared out the side window so Dad couldn't see me cry. He backed the pickup over to the clump of trees and got out. I glanced back to see Dad, the front of him covered in blood, as he loaded the carcass onto the bed of the pickup before covering it with a black tarp, the dead deer's head buckled over its front withers. I was silent all the way home.

"Lorraine, what's the matter?" Mom asked, as I ran in the back door.

"Dad killed a deer. He grazed it and had to hunt it down and shoot it again," I said, as I slammed my bedroom door. I overheard Dad telling Mom what happened.

"Why did you take her hunting?" Mom asked.

"We didn't go hunting. We were riding around in the pickup back on the range."

"You could have come home and gone back later with the boys to look for the buck."

"I wouldn't have found him again. She'll forget about it by tomorrow."

I didn't forget. Dad apologized for upsetting me. Dad got his first deer tag when he was a freshman in high school and killed his first deer at 14. Grandpa had to borrow a gun from his brother because Grandpa didn't have a gun then and he couldn't buy one during World War II. I knew Dad loved to hunt and my brothers liked to hunt too. I just didn't want to know about it or be around when they killed anything.

We grew up with guns in the house. Dad had a gun closet full of pistols and rifles that we were not allowed to touch unless he was with us. Dad taught us to shoot and load guns when we got older, but the only thing I liked to shoot were targets or clay birds.

Dad wore a shoulder holster and carried an automatic .22 around with him on the farm, even when he was driving the tractor. He said he was afraid he might see a coyote or something he wanted to shoot and not have his gun with him. Dad had a license to carry a concealed weapon and knew most of the sheriffs in the county. Plus he always had one of his rifles in the gun rack of his pickup in front of the cab's back window.

Many nights he could be found on the back porch sitting in front of his gun closet cleaning the barrel of one of his rifles, using a long metal rod with small squares of velvety white cloth stuck on the end. Dad reloaded most of his own ammunition and there were lots of empty shells of all different sizes on his reloading bench. First he'd knock out the primer in the bottom of the shell or casing, clean the primer pocket, resize the case with a small instrument and insert a new primer. Then he'd weigh the powder on a small scale according to the chart in his little powder instruction book; the smallest shell, the .22 Hornet, held 11 grams of powder, and the largest shell, the 300 Winchester Magnum, held 83 grams of powder. Once the powder was in the shell, he sealed the bullet on the end by pressing it down into the case with a reloading dye. Like Dad said, "When you want to shoot in a one-inch diameter from 400 yards, everything has to be perfect. You have to reload exactly the same way every time, and of course, you need an accurate rifle." To be a good shot, you have to have a good eye, and my Dad did. There's an old school desk Dad found in the shop that he put out in the rolling hills on the backside of his property. That old desk has been there for years, and it's Dad's favorite place to sit and sight-in his rifles.

Dad loved to hunt, but he loved his land more. As a conservationist, he did everything to protect the land and its natural beauty, and no one had a deeper attachment to the land than my Dad. He rode around the dirt roads for hours, walking through the fields with his dogs, digging in the soil, testing for moisture and minerals. Dad built reservoirs in the valleys of the rolling hills where rainwater collected and stocked the reservoirs with bass. During the winter the reservoirs filled up and during the summer we swam and fished, and Dad planted trees, grass and shrubs around the reservoirs for wildlife habitat. When Dad wasn't working in the fields, we could find him at the pond, as we lovingly called it, putzing around, cutting the grass, watering the trees.

"Let's go fishing in the reservoir," Dad said, with his fishing pole in hand.

We jumped in the back of the pickup, sat on the tailgate with our bare feet swinging in the dust and Dad's white Styrofoam 15-foot boat tied to the top.

"Here, put this fish in the bucket and be careful when you take the hook out of his mouth. You have to twist it like this," Dad said.

"Don't worry, Dad. I can do it by myself," I said.

We fished for hours. "Let's count the fish. Your Mom will be surprised when we get home for dinner. Where's the fish we caught?" Dad asked as he looked in the bucket. "What did you do with them?"

"I threw them back. I knew you were going to kill them and I didn't want to eat them for dinner."

That was the last time I went fishing with Dad for a while.

Dad didn't use the water in the reservoirs for irrigating; he got irrigation water from Clear Lake, sixty miles northwest of the farm. The water was diverted to farmers in the water district through a large canal that curved and twisted through miles of farmland. The canal through Grandpa's farm was thirty feet wide and six feet deep, and when the canal was full the water was swift and smooth as glass. When we finished working in the fields one afternoon, Dad said it was time for us to learn to water-ski.

"Let's go skiing," Dad said.

"We don't have a ski boat," I said.

"Get the skis and the life jackets in the garage and meet me at the bulkhead in the canal."

"You mean those old red plastic water-skis with the torn yellow rubber boots?"

"Yes, and bring your sister and brothers and Mom."

When we got to the canal, Dad was standing on the bank. "The first thing I'll do is tie the rope to the trailer hitch on the pickup. Get the skis and put on the life jacket. Lorraine, you go first," Dad said, as he handed me the jacket.

"Dad, I don't know how to ski."

There were dirt roads on both sides of the canal and Dad stood on the road as he showed me what to do.

"Get in the water and hold the rope between the skis. Bend your knees and crouch over and lean forward and hold on. I'll start slow and the speed will pull you up. As you start to stand up, balance your weight over the skis and hold on. Don't be a fraidy-cat, you can do it. This is the best way to learn to ski, no rough water, no waves and no boats to worry about. Who needs a ski boat?" Dad said. He was right.

There was no room for error. We got up and skied straight down the canal. No tricks, no swerving and no funny stuff or we'd end up on the canal bank. Dad drove and we kids sat in the back of the pickup as lookouts. Thumbs up, go faster. Thumbs down, go slower. By the end of summer, Dad's red plastic skis with the torn yellow rubber boots were ripped apart and we used duct tape to strap our feet into the boots. After working in the fields all day, jumping in the canal was better than taking a cold shower. Dad replaced the yellow rubber boots because Mom insisted. She said one of us was going to break a leg when we fell with skis taped to our feet that wouldn't come off.

Mom was a good water-skier, but she was skinny and self-conscious about wearing a swimsuit. I think it was all the teasing she got in high school. Dad still called her bird legs and that didn't help. One afternoon Mom was on the canal bank wading in the water with Dan, and I was sitting on the bank watching Donna and Joe take turns skiing. Joe got up for the first time and everyone was watching him, except Mom. Dad was driving and watching Joe at the same time.

"Mom. Mom, look out," I screamed. "Mom, look out for the ski rope."

She glanced at me as I jumped up and down, pointing to the pickup. Mom looked at the pickup, saw the rope speeding toward her, grabbed Dan standing in the shallow water and jumped in the canal. Good thing Joe saw Mom in the canal in front of him and let go of the rope.

"Dad, you could have cut Mom in half," I hollered.

Dad jumped out of the pickup and into the canal to help Mom. She was holding on to Dan for dear life.

"Good God, Don. What were you doing? Didn't you see us?" Mom asked.

"I was watching Joe. Thank God you were quick on your feet and figured out what to do."

We were lucky no one got hurt. Mom didn't get over it quite so fast and she didn't come skiing with us again that summer. I heard her give Dad heck that night about being reckless and warned him not to bother coming home if something ever happened to one of us kids.

One of Dad's many dogs

Chapter 9

Our dogs were a source of much happiness and sadness.

When we got up in the morning they were lying on the doormat outside the back door waiting to be petted and fed. The dogs ran free the way dogs should, Dad said. They always jumped in the back of his pickup and rode around with him. Dad was always making a concoction for the dogs to eat out of old deer meat or wild boar, any game he'd left in the freezer so long that Mom refused to cook it. Dad's dogs followed him everywhere and stuck to his side like glue; there was no doubt they liked Dad best, and he named them after playing cards—Ace, King, Jack, Trump, Deuce.

Ace was Dad's favorite dog ever. When Dad was a young boy, he and his father were deer hunting, sitting on the side of a hill on a large rock next to a clump of trees. Ace was sitting a few feet away from Dad; he was a well-trained dog. Grandpa and Dad spotted two bucks moving down the ravine in front of them and waited as the bucks moved closer. Suddenly, a shot rang out across the valley and Dad heard a cry and a whimper. Ace had been shot and blood was everywhere.

There on the crest of the hill in front of them stood two hunters with rifles. Dad told me he tied his shirt around Ace's wound to try to stop the bleeding, but there was nothing he could do. Ace died in Dad's arms.

"Your Grandfather ran to the Jeep and raced down the ravine to confront the hunters. I saw my Dad arguing with the hunters, but after a few minutes he got back in the Jeep. If that had been me,

I would have beaten the hell out of those two men; they were trespassing on our property. They told your Grandfather they saw a coyote in the scope of their rifles and claimed they didn't see us sitting on the rock. I told my Dad that was a bunch of crap; they could have just as well shot one of us. 'What do you mean they didn't see us sitting there with my dog?' I said. But your Grandfather said it was no use arguing with them. The dog was dead and nothing could bring Ace back. Better to leave it alone. I took Ace home and buried him, but I'll tell you one thing, your Grandmother was mad as hell at your Grandfather and didn't speak to him for a week."

It's natural to get attached to your animals. They're helpless creatures, like kids. Our animals became part of our family and went everywhere with us on the farm. After we lost a dog, Dad would bring home a new pup. One time Dad ordered a purebred pup through the mail and named him Deuce, but the puppy had distemper and died not long after he arrived. Dad was mad as hell and thought he should get his money back and Mom said it was his own fault for ordering a puppy through the mail, even though I know she felt terrible the puppy died. When one of our dogs died or got hurt, Dad acted like it didn't bother him, but I knew better. Dad loved his animals and took care of them, just like he did us kids.

One afternoon Dad went hunting with his dog and didn't come home in time for supper. Mom was worried and so was I. It was dark outside. Mom was pacing back and forth in the kitchen, looking out the window that faced the driveway. I glanced out the window and saw lights.

"Dad's home. He's home," I said.

Dad pulled up in the back driveway. He shut off the pickup and sat on the front seat with his head resting on the steering wheel.

"Come on. Let's go see if Dad got a deer," Joe said.

"Boys, wait. Stay here until I come back," Mom said, knowing something was wrong.

Mom got in the pickup and after a few minutes came back in the house and Dad drove away with us kids staring at him from the window.

"Your Dad's going to do the chores," she said. "He's upset. Seems Jack got a hold of one of the poison getters your Dad put out to kill the coyotes. The poison shot down the dog's throat. Dad ran to the stream and shoved water in the dog's mouth to dilute the poison, but Jack died and your Dad buried him in the field. Your Dad's sick those getters killed his dog and he feels responsible."

It took Dad longer than normal to do the chores. I waited up for him and heard him come in. He was sitting in his chair in the den.

"Good night Dad." I stood there and stared at him until he looked up at me. "I'm sorry about Jack, Dad. I wish there was something I could do to make you feel better, to bring your dog back."

"Me too, sweetie," he said, as I put my arms around him and gave him a hug. "I'm afraid there isn't anything anyone can do. He was a great dog." I could see the sad look on my Dad's face and it made me feel sad too.

We had a new puppy a week later.

We prayed together as a family when bad things happened. Dad said his prayers every night and taught us to do the same. There were nights I'd walk by my parents' bedroom and glance through the open door to see Dad kneeling on the floor next to his side of the bed with his rosary beads in his hands, his head bowed, praying. He believed God listened and answered your prayers if you had faith in Him. "Be a good Christian and your reward in heaven will be great," "Dad told us. Mom believed that too; they made a good pair and complemented each other. Dad was conservative and couldn't understand why people didn't agree with him. Mom was realistic and open-minded and knew not everyone was going to share her views. But my Mom and Dad supported each other and stood up for one another; they were a unit.

Not only did we always have a dog, we had cats. None of our animals were ever allowed in the house; they were much happier outside, Dad said. He said we could never have enough cats because they killed the rodents and there were mice, rats and gophers everywhere on the farm. Whenever one of our animals died we had a funeral, made a coffin and buried them outside the fence under a homemade wooden cross with their name on it. I hated it when our animals died, but it didn't seem to bother my cousins.

"Grandma, the cats are fighting again," I said, as we ran through her backyard. "It sounds like they're killing each other in the barn. I can hear them."

"Don't worry about those wild barn cats. They're always fighting with one another. We have too many cats for our own good and they keep multiplying. I told your Grandpa we should give some of them away, but they're so wild we can't catch them," Grandma said.

"I bet we can catch them, Grandma," the boys said.

"You kids stay in the yard and play. I have work to do in the kitchen," Grandma said, as she went in the house.

The next thing I knew the boys were heading toward the barn chasing the cats. "You're going to get in trouble. Grandma said to stay in the yard." I was afraid the boys would hurt the kittens if they caught them, so I ran in the house. "Grandma, the boys are in the barn catching the cats."

"They won't be able to catch those wild cats. If they do, the cats will scratch the heck out of them. Why don't you help me finish making these apple pies? Can you peel the apples?" We lost track of time. After we put the pies in the oven, Grandma went outside to check on the boys.

"What are you boys doing?" Grandma asked, as she walked toward them.

"Nothing, Grandma," they replied, as they stood in front of their sin trying to shield their bad behavior, guilty as hell, looking down at the ground.

"What do you mean 'nothing'? What's behind you? What's in the gunnysack? And what's in the bucket?"

"The sack is moving. I hear kittens crying," I said, as I stood beside Grandma.

Grandma grabbed the top off the bucket. It was half full of water and three kittens were in the bucket crying, barely alive.

"What's the meaning of this?" Grandma asked, as she grabbed the kittens from the bucket. "You boys get in the house right now. I don't ever want you to do anything like this again."

I was crying. Grandma called Mom and made me go home and I don't know what happened to the boys. Mom said Grandpa laid into them.

"Mom, they were trying to drown the kittens in a bucket of water. How could they be so cruel?" I asked.

"Boys will be boys. I'm sure your Grandfather scared them to death," Mom said.

My Grandpa Rominger was always kind to me and I never saw him angry. Dad said that was a good thing.

Grandpa laughed like crazy during the Rangity Tango Kids Show, the talent show all of us kids put on for Father's Day every year we were in grammar school. The show always started with our usual chorus:

> *Rangity Tango, Rangity Tango, Rangity Tango Kids. We're the Rangity Tango, Rangity Tango, Rangity Tango Kids.*

Our family gathered at Grandpa's house in the backyard, sitting on picnic benches on the grass under the sprawling walnut tree. My cousins and I sang, danced, played instruments, performed magic, told funny stories, and roasted our Grandpa and our dads. Grandpa laughed so hard he had tears in his eyes when we imitated him and dressed like him in a long-sleeve, light-blue cotton shirt, farm overalls with suspenders, and a dirty work hat.

One year, Donna and I and Rick and Charlie dressed up like The Beatles, complete with wigs, dark suits, white shirts, guitars and a drum set. We even built a stage and Mom said we looked and sounded just like The Beatles as their record played in the background. We were a talented bunch, or at least we thought so. Grandpa's reaction, rolling back and forth in his chair with his loud, robust, recognizable laugh, was what we all cherished and looked forward to most on Father's Day.

Photo courtesy of *The Winters Express*
Main Street, Winters, California, 1975

Chapter 10

In sixth grade I went to school in town.

There were now thirty kids at Union School in grades one through eight, too many students for one teacher to handle, so the sixth, seventh and eighth graders were transferred to the grammar school in Winters, and I was excited. No more riding my bike to school; I would walk to the end of the lane and catch the bus. Mom took me shopping and bought me a new dress at Weinstock's and I wore white socks and black patent Mary Janes.

"You're going to be the prettiest girl in school and the best dressed," Mom said.

"Mom, Monday is the first day of school and I need your help curling my hair. Grandma doesn't know how to curl my hair."

"I told you weeks ago that your Dad and I were going to be gone the day you start school. We won't be home until Monday night and I'm sorry that happened. We planned the trip and paid for it before the opening day of school was changed. Don't worry. I'll take everything to Grandma's and show her what to do."

The morning of the first day of school at Grandma's was a disaster.

"Grandma, my hair is all curly and sticking up on top. That's not the way Mom fixes it."

"Your Mom brought this bow for you to wear and it matches your dress. We'll put it on top of your hair in the front."

"Grandma, that doesn't look good," I said, as I stared in the mirror with a scowl on my face. I didn't want to cry and make Grandma feel bad, but I didn't want to go to school looking like this.

"You look beautiful. Come on now, we have to go. You don't want to be late the first day of school in town."

I walked into my new class at Waggoner Elementary School with twenty-five kids I didn't know, about to burst into tears. I felt much better when the cutest boy in class introduced himself.

"Hi, I'm Johnny. I think your desk is right behind me," he said.

I forgot about my hideous hairdo until a week later when I brought my class photos home and tried to avoid the subject.

"My teacher's cool, Mom, but he has thick glasses. I don't know how he can see through them. They look like the bottom of Grandma's canning jars and must be half an inch thick. The cutest boy in class sits in front of me and his name is Johnny."

"What's in the envelope? Are those your class photos? Let me see them."

"That bow sitting on top of my head looks like a giant white bug."

They were my worst school pictures ever. The look on my face showed how I felt: ridiculous. Mom apologized more than once for not being home that morning.

"I'm not ordering any of these and giving them to anyone, including Grandma. She'll go on and on about how beautiful I look."

"I don't think they're that bad, and if you ask me, you do look beautiful."

Mom always said that about her children.

One of the best things about going to a much bigger school like Waggoner was after-school sports. It was the first time I played on a team with other girls and I knew this was something I wanted to be good at. All those days of running races on the farm with Dad paid off as I could run faster than all the other girls. I got to play every game even if I wasn't the best player.

This was the year Mom and Dad bought our first set of encyclopedias from a traveling salesman who came to the front door. They were bright blue and had a black stripe on the front with a big black letter; *A* was for all the things and places you wanted to know about that began with the letter *A*. I was fascinated with these encyclopedias and they became my best resource for doing homework, but I was more intrigued by the pictures of places around the world that I'd never seen. I went through every one of those books that year and dreamed about visiting those places. Mom said Winters was a good place to live and grow up. She also said that there was a great big world out there to see and she encouraged us to follow our dreams.

Johnny not only noticed me on the first day, but every day thereafter. It wasn't long before I said to Mom, "Johnny is my boyfriend."

"Your boyfriend. What does that mean?"

"We're going out."

"Going out? Where are you going out to? You're only in sixth grade."

"Oh Mom, you know what I mean. We hang out at school and stuff like that."

"You hang out at school? What do you do when you hang out?"

"We sit together during recess and share our snacks and have lunch together in the cafeteria. You know what hanging out means."

"I don't think I hung out when I was in grammar school."

"Well, then what did you do?"

"I sat with the girls during recess and lunch and we talked about boys."

"I bet I'm having more fun."

"You go to school to learn, not hang out with boys."

"Oh Mom, I'm not hanging out with boys. I'm hanging out with Johnny. Johnny is the most handsome boy in class. The only problem is he's a lot shorter than me."

The day President Kennedy was assassinated I was sitting in the lunchroom with Johnny as a special report came on the television.

"President John Fitzgerald Kennedy has been shot in Dallas, Texas, and was pronounced dead upon arrival at the hospital."

Tears started to roll down my face.

"Don't cry," Johnny said. "There must be a mistake. No one would shoot President Kennedy."

"Look at the television. That's his car racing away from the motorcade and Mom told me this morning the President and Mrs. Kennedy were going to Dallas. I bet Mom is sitting at home in front of the television. She must have seen the whole thing."

The kids in school were upset and the principal closed school for the day. My parents were big supporters of President Kennedy and Mom was crying when she came to pick me up. I had never seen anything like this before, and Mom and I sat in front of the television in the den and cried.

"Mom, why would someone shoot President Kennedy? I don't understand."

"I don't understand either. He has Secret Service men around him and how someone got close enough to shoot him is beyond me."

"What kind of a person would do that?"

"A very disturbed person."

We sat on the couch. Mom's arm was around my shoulder, and I felt her hand move up and down my arm patting it between strokes. It was the first time I understood the word assassinated. *What a senseless act*, I thought.

"There are people in the world who can't help themselves because they're sick. Maybe they didn't have anyone who loved them or maybe they were mistreated. Sometimes people have been so mistreated they don't know the difference between right and wrong, and sometimes they take it out on other people. Nothing is more important than being loved."

Mom held me tight. I knew I was loved, but I was bothered by what happened that day for a long time.

Since I was going to school in town, Momo Cody came by and picked me up if Mom wasn't home after school when I got off the bus. I loved spending the afternoon with her and Popo Cody at the store. One of my favorite things about Popo's store was the hot dogs. I could eat six of them.

"Come here and give your Popo a hug. That's my girl. Do you know how much I love you?"

"Yes I do, Popo, and I love you too. Can I have a hot dog?"

There was a long, glass-enclosed meat counter in the store full of meat and cheese, and the hot dogs were delivered fresh every day. Not the kind of hot dogs that come in a package, but a long strand of link dogs that you cut off one at a time.

"You can have as many hot dogs as you want."

"These are the best hot dogs, Popo," I said, as I dipped the hot dog in a jar of mustard.

"Charles, stop giving her hot dogs. She had a stomachache last week after she left and Shirley said she was sick all night," Momo said.

"I wasn't sick all night, Momo, just half the night." I laughed and looked at Popo and winked, and he winked back.

Popo's brother, Uncle Bill, owned the convenience store, the gas station, a group of cabins on the banks of Putah Creek, and a dance hall where wild and crazy parties went on, according to Popo. The buildings sat on the edge of the creek in one compound across the narrow, two-lane, cement-railed white bridge that crossed into downtown Winters. Cody's Camp was known in the area as a summer resort and people came from miles and miles away to camp on the creek and dance at Cody's Hall.

When I was in high school Putah Creek and Cody's Camp became better known after John and Tom Fogerty spent time at the resort with their families. Their band, Credence Clearwater Revival, had a top hit, "Green River," written about their days at Cody's Camp on Putah Creek.

When I played the song for Momo, she said, "John and Tom spent summers at Cody's campground swimming in Putah Creek and bought groceries and supplies at the store. Popo said those boys were always looking for a good time, if you know what I mean."

"Well, Momo, 'Green River' is the number one song in the country and it talks about Putah Creek, walking along the river road at night, barefoot girls dancing in the moonlight, and it even mentions Great-Grandpa Cody."

"I'm not surprised. Like I said, those boys were always looking for a good time, just like the Cody men."

My Popo Cody and his four brothers were all good looking, worked hard, and partied hard, but not with other women; they were all married and had kids. But they liked their liquor and their card games and were big gamblers. Popo was always rolling dice at the beer counter in the store where his friends gathered after work. He taught me how to throw a good roll. Popo Cody was the most handsome of all his brothers with his tall physique and dark, curly hair.

Momo said Winters hadn't changed much since Theodore Winters founded it in 1875. "A simple town in a complex world. When my friends come to visit, they say it's like going back in time."

There were no stoplights, no fast-food joints, no strip malls, no robberies, no shootings and no drugs dealers. Main Street was two blocks long, wide sidewalks lined with trees and streetlights and stores owned by local families. If you lived in Winters long enough, you knew everyone.

Storefronts along Main Street included the Buckhorn Dining Room & Bar, Western Auto, Smith's Colonial Chapel, Riley's 5-10-15 Cent Store, Ireland Insurance Agency, Roseberry's, Dozier's Drugs, the Bank, Day's Pharmacy, E.J. Graf Ford, the Post Office, Greenwood's Department Store, Maier's TV and Appliance, Taylor's Hardware, Moore's Meat Market, Chulick's Meat Market, Barbi's Beauty Salon, Camile's, Vasey's Grocery Store and Myrna's Café.

Vasey's Grocery Store, was the only grocery in town and customers had charge accounts. Nothing was more fun than walking in the store, getting what we needed and charging it to Mom's account; all I had to do was sign my name. Vasey's had wooden floors, fruit and vegetable bins, and a meat and cheese counter, and one of the Vaseys always waited on me. Greenwood's Department Store, was the only clothing store in town, and at the beginning of every school year, Mom took us to Greenwood's to buy tennis shoes. Greenwood's carried Keds in several colors and it was difficult to decide which color best matched my new school clothes. We got one pair of new shoes at the start of each school year.

Almost every adult who lived in Winters was a farmer, made their living selling things to farmers or worked for farmers. Farming shaped our lives as we grew up, just as it shaped my parents' and grandparents' lives.

For twenty years, Dad grew honeydew melons for a distributor in Woodland. The fruit in the field was picked by hand

and placed on a motor-driven conveyor belt that stretched over ten rows of melons in the field. Once on the belt, the melons were loaded onto trucks and transported to the warehouse. At the end of harvest, hundreds of melons were left in the field because they were too ripe or had sun spots. Dad and I made a deal, that if I picked the melons, I could put up a roadside stand at the end of the lane. Problem was, not that many people drove by my stand four miles out of town and it was hot sitting in the sun during the day waiting for someone to come along and buy a melon or two. Dad said he would talk to the Vaseys and ask if they'd buy the melons. Come to find out, they were happy to buy our fruit, and what a great feeling it was to walk into the grocery store and see my melons in the fruit section for sale.

"You worked so hard this summer," Mom said. "You remind me of your father."

"Dad says if I save enough money I can buy my own car when I'm old enough to drive. I can't wait till I'm older."

Some summers before Dad taught us to drive the farm equipment, Mom, Donna and I cut apricots for our next-door neighbor who had the orchard next to Grandpa's field. The cutting shed was down the lane from our house and we wore our crummiest clothes. After standing on our feet all day surrounded by boxes of apricots, our clothes were sticky and disgusting. Mom was the fastest and taught Donna and me what to do. We held the apricot in one hand and sliced all the way around it with one motion, the pit fell out in the box and we laid the halves down on the tray with one hand and picked up the next apricot with the other. There were twenty-five of us in the shed cutting apricots and we all had a paper card around our necks on a string. Every time the boys brought us a new box full of cots, they punched a hole in our card. I was glad the job only lasted a few weeks. We had to go as fast as we could all day, no dillydallying, as we only made 50 cents a box.

Lots of Mexican field hands worked for Dad during the year, and more during the summer when it was time for harvest. Several of them worked year-round, and took off a couple of months during winter when it rained to visit their relatives in Mexico. Dad was good to "his men," as he called them, paid them well and gave them benefits and insurance. He said he didn't know what he'd do without them. Dad didn't speak much Spanish and they didn't speak much English, but they figured out how to communicate and got along just fine. Once in a while, the workers offered to help me if I was in the field and they were done for the day. Dave, who lived in the bunkhouse with his wife Martha, always seemed to be around at just the right time. Dad said Dave was one of a kind, cared about the farm like it was his own, would do whatever Dad asked him to do and never complained. Martha helped Mom with things around the house.

Dad grew sugar beets, alfalfa, beans, milo, safflower, sunflowers, corn, cotton, rice, barley and wheat, and leased part of his farmland to a tomato grower who grew conventional and organic tomatoes. Every year Dad planted grain on the rolling hills and relied on rain. During severe drought years nothing grew and Dad disked the crops into the ground, or he didn't bother to plant crops on some of his ground. I remember Dad saying, "If we run out of water, where do you think our food is going to come from?" Many years, the tonnage per acre was so poor he barely made enough to pay the bills. Some years, it poured down rain when the crops were blooming, the buds fell off and the fruit didn't set, and some years disease killed the crops no matter how much the crop dusters sprayed. If the alfalfa or oat hay was cut and it rained, the dampness created mildew and Dad got a lot less when he sold the hay, if he could sell it at all.

Dad grew different crops from year to year depending on the price—how much he could get per bushel, per ton or per acre. From year to year he never knew what he was going to get. There was no controlling Mother Nature.

Grandpa Rominger bought farmland before World War II when the price per acre was much less, and he continued to buy land over the years, as did my Dad and Uncle Richard, which helped keep their land debt manageable. Many of the farmers in the county weren't as lucky and couldn't afford to continue farming when years of bad weather put them in debt. It was sad when our neighbors were forced to sell out.

Many of our neighbors attended St. Anthony's, the only Catholic Church in Winters, where we went to mass every Sunday as a family. Dad observed the Sabbath and didn't work on Sundays. Father Coffey was my parents' favorite priest and came to our house every week for dinner. We wrestled with Father on the living room floor and he loved to play games with us and joke around, but most of all Father liked to hunt, just like Dad.

"Shoot Luke, the air's full of pigeons," Dad shouted, when he and Father went bird hunting.

That was Dad's favorite line every time the dogs scared up a bird with Father along on the hunt. All the hunters would stand still with loaded guns, being polite, letting Father shoot first. Dad said his friends thought they'd get to heaven if they were nice to the priest and everyone joked about it. Lots of birds got away and it drove Dad crazy. Father and Dad were constantly arguing about whose shot it was and who had the best hunting dog.

Father was also a horseman and loved to ride.

"Father Coffey bought a retired racehorse named Squeeler. He's a Palomino, 18 hands and runs like the wind," Dad said. "Father's going to board his horse in our barn and maybe if you're lucky you can talk him into riding with you."

Squeeler loved to run and was bigger and taller than Lady who stood 14 hands. It didn't matter where we went for a ride, Lady only wanted to gallop when we turned for home, and all Squeeler wanted to do was gallop from the time we left the barn.

"Father Coffey, let me ride Squeeler today and you ride Lady."

"He's a large, strong horse and you're not used to him, so you'll have to pull back hard on the reins or he'll take off."

Take off he did. I could barely hold him back and had to fight Squeeler the entire ride. It was scary sitting on top of that gigantic racehorse.

Even my Aunt Claire, who was an experienced rider, had a hard time controlling Squeeler. Marilyn, the foreign exchange student who lived with Aunt Evelyne and Uncle Rich, said she was an experienced rider too.

"Marilyn," Dad said, "this horse loves to run. Keep his head down and don't let him get away from you."

Marilyn didn't listen to a word Dad said. The minute she got on Squeeler, he took off in a gallop down the gravel road headed straight for the four-foot wire and wooden fence around our yard. Marilyn was pulling back on the reins as hard as she could, but Squeeler was a racehorse and used to running on an open track.

"Dad, he's not going to jump the fence, is he?" I hollered.

Squeeler started to slide on all four legs and slammed into the fence. The wood popped and splintered as wire crumbled and twisted, flopping down on the grass in front of him. Squeeler was big and powerful and didn't fall, but as he stumbled Marilyn flew over his head.

"Marilyn, are you OK?" Dad yelled, as he ran to help her up.

"I think I am," she said, as she shook herself off. "I couldn't stop him. I thought Squeeler was going to jump the fence."

"He's a racehorse, not a jumper."

"Is Squeeler all right?"

"He seems to be, but we better call the vet to take a look at him. That darn horse hit the fence pretty hard."

Both Marilyn and Squeeler survived the fence and the crash. One thing I knew for sure, I wasn't going to ride that crazy racehorse again. Dad didn't fix the fence; he tore it down. Every time Dad repeated the story, Squeeler was galloping faster and the fence was a foot taller.

"You should have seen that crazy racehorse barreling down the road. It was like he didn't see the fence and put his brakes on with all fours. Busted that five-foot fence in a million pieces and that damn horse didn't even fall. Scared Marilyn half to death and I'm not sure she's ridden the horse since."

The next time Father Coffey came to the house for dinner, Donna backed the old pickup truck we drove into Father's car and smashed in the side of it.

"Dad, you better come out here," Donna said, her voice hesitant.

"What in the heck? How did you do that?"

"I wanted to show Father I learned to drive. I didn't know he parked his car right behind me."

"First you Romingers try to kill my horse and now you crash into my car," Father said, with a chuckle. "Who taught you how to drive, Shorty?"

"Dad did," Donna said.

"Well, that explains it," Father laughed. It wasn't funny, but like Father said, "It's just a car." The next time Father came to visit he parked on the other side of the house.

Dillon Beach, California

Chapter 11

Every summer our family vacationed at Dillon Beach.

Grandpa and Grandma Rominger owned a cabin on the Pacific Coast of California near Point Reyes, just outside the little town of Tomales. Dillon Beach was a small community of summer vacation homes two hours west of Winters, our paradise. The gray brick cabin was nestled in a row of houses beside the narrow, private road separating cabins from the dunes that bordered the beach, leading to the ocean a few hundred yards away.

We packed up the car and took off—Donna, Joe, Dan and I taking turns sitting behind Dad, rubbing his head for 15 minutes for a quarter. It was a sure way to make money to spend at the beach store that had the largest assortment of penny candy we had ever seen. One wall in Lawson's Store, the family that owned the beach, was stacked with tray upon tray of penny candy. For one dollar you could buy 100 pieces.

On the drive to the beach, we stopped in Napa at A&W Root Beer. Dad rolled the window halfway down and the waitress skated up to our car on roller skates, placing her tray on the window and taking our order: one papa burger, one mama burger and four baby burgers with French fries and root beers. Every time we went to the beach, we ate at the A&W. My family was big on tradition.

Grandma and Grandpa bought their first house at the beach when Dad was a kid. Dad and his mother and siblings would spend several weeks at the beach during the summer after harvest was over and Grandpa went deer hunting with his brothers on Goat Mountain. The house sat up on the hill in a village of vacation cabins overlooking the ocean. One hundred cabins were packed together on the side of the hill with a paved road leading to the beach that continued two miles to Tomales Bay where people went crabbing and clamming. Two of Grandpa's brothers, Uncle Todd and Uncle Bill, had cabins at Dillon Beach too. Grandpa and Grandma sold the first house before I started school and built the gray brick house at the bottom of the hill next to the beach. There wasn't a house at Dillon Beach closer to the ocean than Grandpa's. The minute we pulled into the driveway, we jumped out of the car and ran to the beach and I couldn't wait to feel the warm sand between my toes. But the ocean was freezing.

"Don't be a puss," Dad said. "Run in as fast as you can. Wait until the wave is about to break and then dive under it or it'll knock you down."

We got numb fast. We were good swimmers and never wore life jackets, even though there was a strong undercurrent. Dad watched us from the shore as he was a bigger puss; he didn't get in the freezing cold water unless it was absolutely necessary.

Dillon Beach was two miles of soft white sand at the opening of Tomales Bay. "Let's all of us go to the bay and go crabbing," Dad announced.

We bought dead rabbit bait, rented a crab net and headed to the pier. We could only crab during the season and crabs had to be six inches in diameter or we had to throw them back.

"Tie the rope on the net," Dad said. "Hook the rope on the rail of the pier and throw the net out as far as you can. Now we sit."

"Isn't it time to pull in the net?" I asked, standing on the pier freezing in the fog and mist.

"No. Give the crabs time to get the bait," Dad said.

So we waited and stared into the ocean with anticipation, bundled up in our jackets, gloves and boots.

"Pull up the net and let's see if we caught any crabs," Dad said, after waiting for what seemed like an hour.

Dad took the crabs out of the net. If we didn't pick them up by the outer rim of the shell, their pinchers bit us and it hurt. Sometimes we caught a few crabs, but sometimes not a one. When we took them back to the cabin, Dad dropped them into boiling hot water. I refused to eat animals we tortured.

"There's a low tide today and the sand bars are up. Come on, get the boots and shovels and let's go clamming," Dad said.

We rode the clam barge out to the sandbar and walked through the soft sand, carrying our shovels and sinking in the sand up to our knees. When water spurted above the sand, that was the sign a long-necked clam was below. Dad made a competition out of digging and knew what he was doing; the four of us dug, racing like crazy while he supervised. For me, the best thing about digging up clams was the beautiful white clamshell, which I kept, but I hated the taste of clams. The meat was gritty and we got sand in our teeth, no matter how well Mom cleaned them.

Every night after dinner we went for a walk along the beach with the cool ocean breeze blowing in our faces, the soft white sand running between our toes and the waves pounding against the shore. Some nights we walked to the rock cliffs where tide pools filled with starfish, mussels, tigerfish, shell crabs and sea anemones covered the shore.

During low tide, we got up at four in the morning to poke-pole fish or hunt for shells. I loved hunting for shells that had once been home to living creatures before the creatures died and their homes washed up on shore, and my favorite shell was the sand dollar. Lots of times, we didn't see any footprints at the ocean's edge and knew we were the first ones on the beach that morning as we filled our plastic bucket with sand dollars. I never figured out how the flower shape on the top of the sand dollar formed, and even though they all looked the same, each one was different.

"Mom, look at these sand dollars. Can you believe how many I found? They sell them at Lawson's for three dollars, but I'm not going to sell mine," I said, when we got back to the cabin. I kept hundreds of sand dollars.

Dad loved to poke-pole fish and so did the boys. Poke-poles are primitive poles for catching fish that live in tide pools and I'd never seen fish like that; they lived under rocks and looked like they belonged in a science fiction movie. A poke-pole is made from an eight-foot bamboo pole with a metal rod attached to the end with duct tape. On the end of the eight-inch metal rod was a large hook that we baited and then waded out to the tide pools, poking the poles under the rocks. The fishing part wasn't much fun and we didn't catch many fish, but the excursion with Dad, my sister and brothers at four in the morning in the dark, carrying our poles down the beach over the rocks, singing songs, slipping on seaweed and trying not to fall in the freezing cold water, that was what poke-pole fishing was all about.

"These are the best tide pools and there's no one around. Let's get the bait on the hooks and catch us some fish," Dad said.

"I'm freezing, Dad, and I'm all wet," I said.

"I told you not to wear those shoes. Why didn't you climb over the rocks and not get in the water? Stick the pole in that tide pool and wait." It was dark outside and we had to use our flashlights until the sun came up.

"I slipped on the seaweed and scratched my leg on the rocks and fell in the water. My leg is bleeding," I said.

"Stand in the water and it'll stop the bleeding," Dad said.

110

"But the water's freezing."

"Dad, I caught something. It's orange and looks like a monster and it's all thorny," Joe said.

"That's not good to eat. Throw him back," Dad said.

"I'm cold," Dan said.

"Stop complaining," Donna said. "This happens every time." And so the morning would go, with Dad trying his best not to lose his patience.

"How many fish did you catch?" Mom asked, when we got back to the cabin.

"Not a one, Mom, but we had a good time," Joe said. "Dad's good at finding tide pools with fish we can't keep." Everyone laughed, but Dad.

At night we made a fire and roasted marshmallows and squished them between graham crackers with chocolate squares. Some nights we played cards, checkers and dominoes. We were a competitive bunch and loved to play games.

"Joe, I'm not playing with you again. You cheat; no wonder you always win. You change the rules as we play the game and it's not fair," Dan said, as he threw his cards on the table.

"That's enough, you kids. Time for bed," Dad said.

The four of us slept in the back bedroom with bunk beds. Donna and I got the top bunks and the boys slept on the bottom. They didn't like that, but we came along first and had dibs on the top. The two top bunks had wooden ladders to climb up and the boys thought because they were boys, they should get to sleep on the top. That was one argument they didn't win; Donna and I had staked our claim to the top bunks long ago.

During the summer, Dad was busy with harvest and went to the farm during the week and came to the beach on weekends. The time went by fast and we did something different every day. There was no television, no stereo and no phone at the beach house and Grandma and Grandpa wanted it that way. This was a place to get away and spend time with family. Every couple of days we used the pay phone at the store to call home and check on Dad.

Grandpa bought us an old surfboard from the Lawson boys who lived at the beach and surfed every day. Surfing was harder than it looked and we didn't have anyone to teach us, so we taught ourselves. Mom spent hours on the beach watching us, but she didn't swim. She said the water was too cold and Dad refused to buy wetsuits.

"You kids are tough and wetsuits are for sissies," he said. We'd come out of the water blue from the cold, shaking all over with our teeth chattering, but it didn't matter.

The dunes lined the beach for two miles and we spent hours playing hide-and-seek.

"Mom, we can't find Dan," I hollered one day, as I ran in the house.

"What do you mean?" Mom asked, with fear in her voice.

"We've been playing hide-and-seek and we can't find him. We called and called and I think he might be lost in the dunes and doesn't know how to get back to the house. After a while all the dunes look the same," I said, as we headed to the beach.

"Dan, Dan, where are you?" we hollered, as we ran through the dunes.

"You don't think Dan would go into the ocean by himself, do you?" Mom asked. "You know Dan isn't a good swimmer and he doesn't understand how dangerous the undercurrent is."

"Mom, we'll find him," I said. "Don't worry. We'll find Dan."

"He's the youngest and can't take care of himself the way you kids can. Let's split up and look for him. Lorraine, you go to the beach, and Donna you go out to the road that leads to the campground and I'll look through the dunes with Joe. Is this where you kids were playing?"

"No, it wasn't," I said.

"Yes, it was," Donna said.

"No, it was over there, Mom," Joe said.

"No wonder you kids got lost. These dunes do look the same. Holler if you find him." Mom was frantic.

We looked and looked and Mom thought we should go to the store and call the police. As we walked over the crest of a dune, beyond in the campground we saw Dan playing with a bunch of kids.

We ran to him. "Dan, we've been looking all over for you, you scared us half to death. What are you doing here?" Mom asked.

"I was playing. Joe and Donna and Lorraine ran away from me and I couldn't find them."

"Come with me, let's go home," Mom said, as she looked at us with that look in her eyes. I knew what was coming and I was in no hurry to get back to the cabin.

"I'm upset with you big kids. Your brother is too young for you to leave him alone in the dunes. I don't ever want you to let him out of your sight again. Do you hear me?"

"We were playing hide-and-seek," Donna said, looking at Mom with her hands on her hips. "We didn't run off and leave him alone on purpose."

For the next several days we didn't let Dan out of our sight, but we blamed him for getting us in trouble. He was the one who disappeared and we got the axe.

Indian Mountain looked like an oversized anthill covered with sand and was the tallest peak at Dillon Beach. Two miles from the cabin and a steep, uphill climb, we attempted to reach the top every time we went for a hike.

"Dad, why do they call this Indian Mountain?" I asked, as we climbed to the top.

"Hundreds of years ago, Indians lived here on the coast and Indian Mountain was their hunting ground. I've found arrowheads on this mountain since the time I came here as a kid. If you see a break in the smooth sand, take a close look. It could be an arrowhead."

"It could be lot of things, Dad," I said. "How do you know the Indians hunted on this mountain?"

"Your Grandfather told me and he knows. He was friends with the family who bought this land nearly 100 years ago."

"Well, then how come we've never found an arrowhead?" Joe asked.

"You're not looking hard enough," Dad said.

"I think that's an old wives' tale," I said.

Dad took us to Indian Mountain to hunt for arrowheads every time we came to the beach and Dad knew we'd find one, someday. We haven't yet.

On Fourth of July there was a bonfire on the beach and everyone pitched in and gathered driftwood. Most of the kids who hung out during the summer stayed at the beach in their families' cabins like we did. The cute surfer boys who surfed all day picked up girls at night and had a different girl every week. I liked one of them and I wanted him to pick me up, but he never paid one bit of attention to me. I was tall for my age and most of the boys were shorter than me. Seemed like the beach boys only wanted to pick fights with Donna and me.

"Here come the Rominger girls. It's the Jolly Green Giant and her tagalong sister."

114

"You're just a bunch of bullies," Donna said, as we sat our surfboard on the sand.

"Where did you get that giant old-fashioned surfboard? Can't your old man afford to buy you a new one?" the boys asked, as they kicked sand on our surfboard.

"I'm going to kick the shit out of them," Donna mumbled under her breath to me. "Leave us alone or you'll be sorry."

"Yeah, right. Your sister has the hots for Chris and everyone knows it, but he wouldn't touch her with a 10-foot pole. She's twice as big as he is," the boys laughed.

"Get away from us and stop kicking sand on our surfboard," Donna said.

"It's old and beat up and one more scratch won't make any difference," one of the boys said, as he ran his foot across the top.

"Get away from our board," Donna said, as she stood in front of him with her face in his. "I'm not moving until you apologize for scratching our surfboard."

"Don't you think you're tough? I could knock you flat with one punch."

"Shut up, you dummy," Donna said.

"Who's calling who a dummy?" he asked, drawing a line in the sand with his foot. "Come on, Miss Tough Girl. Step across this line and see what happens to you."

"I'm not afraid of you," Donna said, as she stepped across the line.

As she did, Bill pushed her and she fell backward on the sand. Donna jumped up and punched him in the face, hitting him so hard he landed flat on his butt.

"Come on, Bill. Gonna let a girl knock you down?" the boys laughed.

Bill took a swing at Donna and missed and she punched him again with her right hand and didn't even flinch. The next thing I knew they were going at one another and the boys were egging them on...me too.

"Hit him again," I yelled.

Bill took a beating, backed away and said, "I ain't fighting no girl. Stay away from me or you'll be sorry. Come on guys, let's go."

"Bill, gonna let a girl beat you up?" the boys laughed.

"I could kill her if I wanted. I was playing nice. I'm out of here," Bill said.

"You kicked his ass," I said. "Way to go, sis. That'll show him." I was proud of my sister. I knew she was tough.

"Donna, what happened to your shirt?" Mom asked, as we walked in the cabin door. "What happened to your head? You've got sand all over your face and blood in your hair. Are you OK?"

"Donna beat the shit out of those boys on the beach," I said.

"Lorraine, watch your mouth. Donna, get over here. My God, what have you done? Don, I want you to go to the beach and find those boys," Mom said, as she turned and motioned to Dad.

"You should have seen that boy take off. Donna kicked his ass."

"Donna, what have I told you about fighting?" Dad asked.

"I didn't hit him first, Dad. He hit me first. You always said, never start a fight. But if someone hits you first, finish it. Well, I finished it."

"That's right, Dad. That boy hit Donna first."

"I hope you showed him a thing or two," Dad chuckled.

"Don, what a thing to say in front of your girls," Mom said, in disgust.

"Oh, come on, Mom. Those boys had it coming and I'm glad I was on the beach with Donna. Problem is, they'll never get near us again."

"Oh yeah, guess why that's a problem?" Donna said. "Lorraine has a crush on one of them and he just happens to be six inches shorter than she is."

"He is not six inches shorter than I am. He's just a little shorter."

"Both of you need to stay put for a while," Mom said. "I think we've had enough excitement for one day."

Donna and I went in the bathroom to take a shower. Mom was upset.

"Don, teaching those girls to fight is not a good idea. They're going to be teenagers and I don't want the girls picking fights with boys," Mom said.

"You don't have to worry about Lorraine picking any fights, but Donna, boy is she tough. Getting in a fight in the middle of a group of boys, guess I don't have to worry about her taking care of herself."

"When she gets in a fight with a boy twice her size and comes home with a bloody face and a broken nose, I'll let you deal with it."

"Don't worry, Mom," Donna yelled from the bathroom. "I may be tough, but I'm not stupid." We looked at each other laughing, our mouths covered with our hands.

Little did those boys know that my Dad spent hours teaching us to box. He was a boxer in college and a darn good one. Dad showed us to punch with both fists and protect our face with one hand while punching with the other. He walked around the house trying to pick a fight, begging us to hit him so he could show off. Donna and I happened to come along first and it didn't matter that we were girls. Dad wanted us to be able to "hold our own." When we were kids, I fought with my sister and I was much taller than she was. Dad said Donna learned to fight to protect herself from me. When we were little and Mom told me to watch her, I had no choice but to drag her around because she couldn't keep up. Donna had years of being picked on to make up for.

We nicknamed the cabin the broom shack and when we got ready to go home, Mom spent hours cleaning. One time the vacuum broke, so we swept the indoor outdoor carpet with a broom and Mom didn't think it was funny. She liked to leave the cabin cleaner than we found it and didn't want anyone in the family saying we didn't clean up the place. It never failed that someone would complain to Grandma if they found the house in a mess and then the whole family knew about it. But Mom never complained to Grandma; she never complained to anyone. She'd just clean the house until it was spotless and taught us to do the same.

Right before we walked out the door we signed the guestbook and if we forgot to sign the book we heard about that too. Grandma knew who was at the beach, and signing the guestbook was a ritual. We all sat down at the kitchen table and took turns writing a paragraph about our days at the beach. Our family was big on traditions, traditions we still keep.

When our vacation at the beach ended, we returned to the farm and Donna and I flew on the airplane to visit Auntie Lona, who lived in Pasadena in southern California. We stayed with her for a week every summer we were in grammar school, like clockwork. Mom took us shopping and bought us a new outfit to wear on the plane. Flying on the plane by ourselves was a big deal.

"Watch your sister, Lorraine. Don't let her out of your sight. Be good girls and do what Auntie tells you. Don't talk to anyone except the stewardess until you see Auntie at the gate," were Mom's last words as we boarded the plane.

"Don't worry Mom, I'll watch her," I said, grabbing for her hand. Donna didn't need taking care of, but I was the oldest and that was my job. Donna looked at me, pulled her hand away and rolled her eyes.

"Don't touch me. I can take care of myself much better than you can."

Going to visit Auntie was going to Hollywood where all the rich, famous, beautiful people lived, where the movie stars lived. Auntie looked like a movie star in her beautiful clothes and jewelry and she was always dressed up, much different than the way we dressed on the farm. Auntie had left Winters and moved to Los Angeles to work for a famous doctor as his office manager.

"Where do you girls want to go first?" Auntie asked.

"Disneyland, Disneyland!"

"Let's go on the Matterhorn first. It's our favorite ride and we love to go fast."

Auntie waited for us at the exit of each ride and we counted the number of rides we could do in a day. First Disneyland, then Knott's Berry Farm and Olvera Street, where Donna and I picked out a handblown glass animal made in front of us by a street vendor. We watched in fascination as the glass melted and took the shape of the animal we selected. I kept my dogs and horses, wrapped in tissue, in a special memory box.

One summer, Mom came with us on the plane so she and Auntie could visit their first cousin, Patty, who lived in Pacific Palisades. Patty married John Graham, the nephew of Elizabeth Arden and heir to her cosmetic company. Patty's mom and my Mother's mom were sisters.

"Mom, is this her house?" I asked, looking out the car window. "I've never been inside a house like this. She must be rich."

We drove through a big circular driveway with colored flowers along the edge and a fountain in the center surrounded by grass. The mansion was three stories tall with gigantic, black double front doors.

"This looks like a castle in Disneyland," I said.

"Girls," Mom said, in a matter-of-fact way standing at the front door, "I want you to be on your best behavior." She stared at both of us. "Be polite, sit on the couch like ladies and for God's sake, don't touch anything. Patty thinks we're her country cousins. Let's show her we are not hicks from the sticks." Mom raised her eyebrows and winked.

Mom lived on a farm, but she had style and taste and appreciated beautiful things. I watched Mom looking around as we walked to the door. She was taking in every little detail as she rang the doorbell. A woman in a black dress with a white apron opened the door.

"Hello, I'm Shirley. This is my sister Lona and these are my girls. We're here to see Patty."

"Yes, come in and I'll let Mrs. Graham know you're here. Please wait in the living room."

"Thank you," Mom said.

"Who was that?" Donna asked, twirling around and looking up at the ceiling.

"The maid," Mom said. "Stand still."

"You mean they have servants?" I asked.

"Shhh," Mom said. "Just wait and don't touch anything."

The front entry led to a room the size of our house with black marble floors and mirrors everywhere. Each way I turned I could see myself, and when I looked up, the ceiling was so high I could see the entrance to the rooms on the second floor. The rooms opened to a second-floor landing that looked down on the living room, and in the corner of the room was a long, wide, winding staircase. It was the longest banister I'd ever seen.

"Mom, can we slide down the banister?" Donna asked, as she started to walk toward the stairs.

"Get back here."

The furniture was black and gray and covered in velvet, and the room was full of glass tables, black velvet chairs, couches and crystal chandeliers. The tables were covered with crystal dishes and glass art objects.

"Don't touch that," Auntie said, as I reached toward a glass bowl. "It probably cost more than my car."

"Have you ever seen such a house in your life?" Mom whispered to Auntie.

"Lona. Shirley. Well, if it isn't my cousins from the country," Patty said. "These must be your girls?"

"Hello, Patty," Mom said, as she reached out her hand to Patty and Patty shook Mom's hand.

Patty turned toward Donna and me.

"Hello, I'm Lorraine."

"I'm Donna."

"So girls, tell me, how do you like Los Angeles? I bet you don't see things like this on the farm," Patty said.

"We've been to Los Angeles lots of times and we love Disneyland," Donna said, with a smirk in her voice. "But I like the farm the best."

"I bet you do," Patty said.

"Patty, are your children home?" Mom asked, trying to change the subject.

"No, they're at boarding school," Patty said.

I knew right then and there we were not getting off the couch the entire visit. I wanted to run through the mansion, peek in every room and slide down the banister. So did Donna and it was all we could do to sit still. The maid brought us some lemonade and cookies and we waited while Mom and Auntie made small talk with Patty.

"I don't think she liked us very much, Mom," I said, as we got in the car.

"Yes, she does," Auntie said. "She just lives in a different world than we do."

"Yeah," Mom said. "Look at the way she lives in a mansion with maids, a cook and a chauffeur. Can you imagine what she'd think if she came to the farm with all the dust and dirt?"

"And flies and mice," I said.

"I'll take the farm," Donna said.

"Me too," I said. "Not much fun living in a house where you can't touch anything. I bet she doesn't have to clean her room on Thursdays or do the dishes or clean the garage on Saturday."

"Doing chores is part of growing up and it teaches you to be responsible," Mom said. "Auntie and I had chores to do when we grew up. It's part of life."

"It's not part of Patty's life," I said.

I dreamed about the mansion for months and what it would be like to live there. I decided when I grew up I was going to live in a mansion and have lots of servants to do my chores.

Rominger Mud Bowl, circa 1970s

Chapter 12

Thanksgiving was a feast at my Great-Uncle Bob and Aunt Mildred's.

We spent the day eating, drinking, playing cards and touch football. It was the day to give thanks for all God's gifts. Forty of us crammed into the living room seated at a 30-foot, L-shaped table. I always ate too much and wished I could throw up after dinner, but I never figured out how to stick my finger down my throat.

My favorite part was dessert—miniature ice-cream turkeys and coconut-covered snowballs that Aunt Mildred ordered special from the ice-cream shop. The ice-cream turkeys stood six inches tall, decorated with colored frosting that crackled every time I stuck it with the spoon and took a bite.

After dinner the men played pinochle. We all learned to play card games when we were old enough to hold a deck of cards. The kids teamed up for touch football on the front lawn and not a Thanksgiving went by that one of us didn't break a bone.

Christmas was my favorite holiday of the year and as Catholics we celebrated the birthday of Jesus Christ, our savior, who came into the world to teach us to love one another, the greatest gift of all. We prepared for Christmas for weeks, making pies, cookies, breads and candy, decorating the house, putting up the tree and wrapping presents. Our best gifts were the homemade ones and I loved to sew and make ties for my grandfathers. My tag, "Made especially for you by Lorraine," was sewn into every gift, and my grandfathers said their ties were one of a kind.

On Christmas Eve our family gathered at Popo and Momo Cody's house in Winters and after dinner we attended midnight mass. Dad fell asleep and Mom pinched him the entire mass to keep him awake. Momo Cody had the prettiest Christmas tree and it filled the living room, covered with colored glass bulbs, lights and crumpled silver icicles. As a child, I remember Momo putting the same decorations on her tree year after year and wrapping her glass bulbs in paper, neatly packed in a box in her hall closet.

"Momo, can I help you decorate your tree?" I asked, every Christmas.

"Of course you can, but you have to put the icicles on the very edge of each branch one at a time, like this."

I'd last for 10 minutes; it was tedious work. Besides, the minute I left the room, Momo redid all the branches I decorated. Her Christmas tree was her pride and joy.

"We might as well leave it up until the end of January. We spend all this time getting ready for Christmas and it's over in twenty-four hours. Do you have any idea how long it takes me to decorate the tree?" Momo asked.

"No, Momo," even though I knew the answer.

"Twelve hours, twelve long hours, and have you ever seen a more beautiful tree?"

"No, Momo," I said, every year. "Never."

The most treasured gift I got for Christmas was a *Little Women* doll that resembled the sister, Jo, that Popo Cody bought me when I was five.

"Popo, she is the most beautiful doll I've ever had and you are the best Popo ever," I said, as I wrapped my arms around his legs. "I love you this much," stretching my arms straight out from my shoulders as far as I could. I looked up at my Popo, smiling, as he bent down, picked me up and held me in his arms.

"She's a very special doll for my very special girl."

Not long after Popo gave her to me, I cut off her long, dark hair with a pair of scissors and threw her hair in the burning garbage behind our garage. Her hair was hard to comb and the more I combed, the more the hair fell out. I butchered her hair with the most awful, uneven haircut, exposing part of her scalp.

"I can't believe you cut off her hair. Your grandfather gave you this doll and do you know how much he paid for her? I told him you weren't old enough for a doll like this, but he insisted on buying it for you," Mom said. She was furious.

"Well," I said, "you cut off all my hair."

I wanted long hair, but grew up with a pixie cut and I remembered why.

"If you won't let me comb the tangles out of your hair," Mom said, day after day, "then we'll have to cut it off."

And cut off my hair she did.

When I was in college, I took the doll to a doll restorer and replaced her long dark hair and sat her on my bed in her original clothes. I've often wondered if at five years old I cut off Jo's hair to get back at Mom for cutting off mine. I remember in the book *Little Women*, Jo cut off her hair for money to buy gifts for her family.

Christmas morning, bright and early, we went to Grandma and Grandpa Rominger's house. Dad's siblings and my cousins arrived at 8:00 a.m. sharp. No one missed Christmas morning at Grandma's. The best thing about Christmas breakfast was the fresh, homemade link sausages we made from the pigs Dad had butchered the week before. Having our own chickens and cows, we had fresh eggs, butter, cream and milk. The food covered the 30-foot rectangular table stretching from one end of the dining room into the adjoining bedroom, steam rising from the plates of food carrying the smells throughout the house. Grandpa Rominger sat at the head of the table, his sons next to him with their wives, his daughters and their husbands, great aunts and uncles and kids in-between, with Grandma at the opposite end of the table.

"Grandma, is it time to open presents?" the kids asked. "Not yet, we haven't had our special homemade treats." Warm and straight out of the oven, nothing was better than Grandma's hot cross buns, apple cake and pecan rolls.

Pecan Rolls

1-1/2 cups milk, scalded
1-1/2 cups sugar
4 tsp salt
3/4 cup shortening
5 packages yeast
2 cups warm water
6 eggs, beaten
15–16 cups flour
Syrup
1 cup butter
3 cups brown sugar
1/2 cup light corn syrup
3 cups pecans

Scald the milk. Add sugar, salt and shortening. Cool to lukewarm. Dissolve yeast in warm water. Stir in lukewarm milk, beaten eggs and half the flour. Beat. Work in remaining flour. Knead for 8 minutes and roll out dough in a rectangle. Combine and melt syrup ingredients, let cool and pour over dough. Roll dough into a round loaf and cut in one-inch slices. Place rolls flat in pie plate. Leave space between rolls as dough will rise. After dough rises place additional pecans on top. Bake at 350 for 20 minutes or until golden brown. Watch the dough, as it easily burns on the bottom if cooked too long.

The girls cleared the dishes while the adults snuck into the living room, cameras in hand. Dad's movie camera was old-fashioned with a film reel that made a clicking noise as it turned and recorded. Two huge lights covered with metal domes lit up the room and blinded us if we glanced at the camera. The kids lined up by age, the youngest first, and I was first once, but too little to remember. As the door opened, one by one we rushed into the room, pushing each other, looking for the Christmas tree in the corner surrounded by presents that covered the floor.

Grandma and Grandpa sat in their chairs on each side of the tree like the King and Queen overseeing court. Grandma's tree was decorated with homemade ornaments, cranberry and popcorn strings, colored lights, and a gold star on top, much different than Momo Cody's tree. As my cousins were born, the fireplace mantel was lined with seventeen hand-knit Christmas stockings, tacked to the wooden mantel with each of my cousins' name on one. Aunt Evelyne made all the kids a stocking for our first Christmas, another Rominger tradition. The stockings were filled with all kinds of goodies: marbles, a ping-pong paddle and a quarter from Aunt Edith, Grandma's sister. One by one, starting with the youngest, we opened our presents in the center of the room with everyone watching. It was our Christmas ritual and took four hours.

"Christmas comes but once a year and I want to see everyone's presents. There's no rush, we have all day," Grandma said every Christmas.

Except for occasional trips to the kitchen to reload the dishes and start preparing Christmas dinner, we sat on the floor, oohing and aahing at every gift, laughing and eating See's candy. There was nowhere else I'd rather be than in Grandma's house on the farm with my family on Christmas Day. I waited hours for Grandma and Grandpa to open their presents because they were the oldest and went last.

Grandpa was tall and stout, a big German with huge weathered hands; one could tell he was a farmer by his hands.

"Here Grandpa, open my gift. I made this especially for you."

"If that isn't the most handsome tie I've ever seen." I always knew he loved it because the next time I saw him in a suit he'd have on the tie. He wore a tie I made for him the day I got married.

As was tradition, we were not allowed to take our stocking off the mantel until we finished opening our gifts. I remember the excitement as we dumped the contents on the floor, madly searching for the quarter Aunt Edith put in all our stockings.

For years, Grandma gave each of us a ping-pong paddle, with a red rubber ball attached on a long, sturdy rubber string. All day we had contests to see who could hit the ball the most times in a row, but I never won. Joe and Dan beat me every year and could hit more than 100, easy. Rick and Charlie and Bruce were pretty good at it too, and the five of them would stand in Grandma's big entry hall and compete for hours. Rick and Joe usually won. It wasn't long before the rubber string broke and Joe stole my paddle and tried to make me think it was his. He didn't fool me, but I let him think he did.

In the entry room was a straight wooden staircase that led to the second floor and we kids took turns dropping the marbles from our stockings down the stairs. The noise from hundreds of marbles dropping and bouncing down the wooden staircase, faster and faster, louder and louder, sounded like a heavy hailstorm pounding on a tin roof.

"Kids, enough with the marbles. Put the marbles away," the adults yelled.

I never understood why they gave us marbles in our stockings year after year.

The year we kids sang "Oh Christmas Tree, Oh Christmas Tree" to Grandpa in German was a year to remember. We practiced for weeks. Both his parents were born in Germany and Grandpa was proud of his heritage.

"Grandpa, we have a surprise for you," I said, when he finished opening his presents. I motioned my cousins to the center of the room, walked to the piano against the wall and began to play as we all sang...

O Tannenbaum, O Tannenbaum,
Wie treu sind deine Blatter.

O Tannenbaum, O Tannenbaum
Wie treu sind deine Blatter.
Du grunst nicht nur zur Sommerzeit
Nein auch im Winter wenn es schneit.
O Tannenbaum, O Tannenbaum
Wie true sind deine Blatter.

I won't forget the smile on Grandpa's face when his grandchildren finished the song. His eyes were watering and I knew he loved it even though he never said much. Grandpa was a man of few words and my Dad was just like him.

"Merry Christmas, Grandpa," I said, as I put my arms around him.

"The best present ever," he whispered.

After dinner the men set up card tables and chairs in the entry room and played pinochle and the women cleaned up the mess.

The day after Christmas, we returned to Grandma's house for turkey sandwiches, followed by the annual Rominger Mud Bowl. If it didn't rain, the boys watered the equipment field next to Grandma's house with the water truck. The girls were the last ones to get picked, except Donna and my cousin Corinne, the two tough girls in the family. It was tackle football, no whining, no crying, no whimpering and no babies. By the time the game ended, we were covered with mud from head to toe and couldn't tell who was who in the photos. More than one of us was bruised, limping or pissed off. We weren't good losers; all of us played to win. Some Christmases our second cousins from back East came for the holiday and there were plenty of kids to make up the teams.

Once, as we hosed ourselves off after the Mud Bowl, we noticed flames spiraling into the air from across the road, and rushed into Grandma's house. "Call the fire department. Call the fire department. Aunt Evelyne and Uncle Richard's house is on fire!"

Flames roared 20 feet high through the broken windows, the house ablaze, as we ran to do something, anything. There was nothing to do but stand there and watch as the fire took control and flames raced through the home. First we were all in shock and then we were all in tears. They'd left the Christmas tree lights on and the firemen determined that a short in the cord started the fire. We did have something to be grateful for that Christmas; no one was home when it burnt to the ground.

Mom's favorite holiday was Easter, the day Christ rose from the dead to save us. We were raised to believe in God, to live in his likeness and treat others as we wanted to be treated. "Love your neighbor as yourself," Mom often said.

We covered dozens of colored eggs with decorations from Mom's craft box and each of us had a special egg with our name on it from the Easter Bunny, or so Mom told us. We believed in the Easter Bunny until we saw Mom without her mask and ears. She'd dress in a white, furry bunny costume with a bunny tail and run around the yard hiding presents in our Easter nests that we made in Grandma's yard with alfalfa. Even though we knew the presents weren't from the Easter Bunny, we kept Mom's secret. On Easter morning we lined up, youngest first, to run down Grandma's front porch steps into the yard and claim our nests with an Easter basket full of candy.

"Time for the Easter egg hunt," Grandma said, and the hunt was on.

Easter eggs were hidden in the trees, shrubs, flowers, on the fence, in every nook and cranny in the yard. Grandma hid dozens of eggs and we collected most of them, but there were always a few eggs too well hidden that the dogs found days later.

Momo Cody bought Donna and me a new Easter dress each year we were in grammar school with matching shoes, purse, hat and gloves. The dresses were pink, the hats covered with flowers and ribbons, complete with white patent shoes and socks with lace trim. It was fine when I was little, but as I got older, I felt like I was playing "dress up" and I was self-conscious of the thick black hair on my legs. I wasn't a little girl anymore.

"OK," Mom said, "you can shave your legs for Easter, but be careful with the straightedge razor and use lots of soap in the tub."

On Easter morning I heard Dad comment first, as I walked down Grandma's front steps into the yard. "What in the world is wrong with Lorraine's legs? It looks like she walked through a minefield."

"I told her she could shave her legs," Mom said.

"Why in the world would you do that?"

"She's begged me for a year and I got tired of saying no. She's self-conscious of the dark hair on her legs. It's bad enough my mother insists she wear those frilly, baby girl dresses, but I had no idea she'd cut herself to death."

I wanted to run and hide. The skin on my legs was cut to the bone with two long, narrow strips of red raw skin exposed between my ankle and knee. The cuts bled all night and I couldn't decide what looked worse, the sores or the row of Band-Aids. There I was in my ridiculous baby girl dress with blood oozing down the front of both legs and Mom insisting no one noticed.

"What happened to your legs?" Joe asked, pointing and laughing. "That looks ugly."

"Shut up and leave me alone. It hurts and I know how ugly it is. I don't need you making fun of me too."

I knew everyone was looking at me, but when I looked at Dad he had a smile on his face and winked and motioned to me to stand next to him. I didn't shave my legs again for months and the hair grew back thicker and blacker.

"There would be no Easter or Christmas without the birth and death of Jesus," Mom said. "We give presents to the people we love, much like the Three Wise Men gave presents to Jesus, but getting presents is not what Christmas or Easter is about. It's about our faith in God and his teachings, to live our lives in his likeness and love one another."

After Easter morning at Grandma's, it was off to the hills for the Rominger Easter Picnic as we loaded the pickups with tables, chairs, food and baseball equipment. Everyone loved going to the hills on the back side of Grandpa's farm to the sprawling, lush green meadow surrounded by rolling hills covered in oak trees, hidden from the world, our protected hideaway. Grandpa, Dad and Uncle Richard gathered up most of the stuff and all of us kids helped. Some years, we had close to 100 people at the Easter picnic, including our extended family from Sacramento and lots of friends from Winters. Two of my cousins picked teams for baseball and everyone got to play, even the little kids who could barely hold the bat, let alone hit the ball. They got lots more strikes than the rest of us and it went on and on and on. Us bigger kids just stood in the outfield, waiting and complaining to each other. I think we forgot that we were the little kids a few years before. Grandpa and my great-uncles, the old guys in the bunch, pitched and no one complained. They were really good pitchers.

On one side of the meadow was a small, dry creek bed where we hunted for salamanders, orange lizard-like animals with velvety skin. We never brought them home because if we did, they'd die. We found hundreds of animals growing up on the farm, but only brought them home if they were hurt and needed care. Putting wild creatures in a box or cage was cruel.

The picnic area was several miles from our house back in the hills and across a sandy creek to the meadow. It never ceased to amaze me how poorly city people drive when they get off-road.

134

"No problem, we'll get to the picnic just fine," our friends said. "Your Mom drew us a map."

But without fail, someone got stuck, took a wrong turn, slid off the road into the field or buried their truck to the axle in the sand crossing the creek bed. Dad said city people didn't know how to drive and he was right. Never a family Easter picnic passed that we didn't pull someone out of the field or the creek bed with the wench on the pickup.

"Thank God I taught you kids to drive in the mud and dirt and change a tire," Dad said. "Don't think your old man doesn't know a thing or two."

Mule-drawn wagons, circa 1915

Sidehill harvester, circa 1921

Chapter 13

I hated being taller than all the boys in my eighth-grade class.

I liked to dance, but dreaded the school dances because Johnny was a head shorter than me and our classmates teased us. Mom insisted I take dance lessons and learn to dance and she insisted it would boost my confidence.

"Ballroom dancing?" I asked. "What kind of dancing is that?"

"It's the latest craze. I signed you up for lessons with some of the girls in your class. You're too self-conscious about being tall and this will be good for you. You'll learn to follow a boy's lead and I'm sure there will be boys in class taller than you."

Classes were held in an auditorium with hardwood floors, and chairs lined the perimeter of the room. The teacher was a heavyset woman, nicely dressed and well groomed, and when she finished taking roll she instructed the girls to line up. She told us to hold out our hands, palms down, and she proceeded to walk down the line with a long, thick wooden ruler.

"I expect you to dress appropriately, be prepared for class and pay attention at all times. I'm sure you read the packet of information that was sent to you explaining the rules of the class," she said.

Shit, I'm in trouble, I thought. *Mom never said anything about the rules.*

"Hands play an important part in dancing since you hold your partner with them and lead with them."

The first thing I remember was the ruler hitting the ends of my fingers. Those were the good old days; teachers would never get away with that today.

"Your nails need to be manicured. Remember that next week."

What a bitch, I thought. I couldn't believe Mom forgot to tell me the rules. She knew I'd resist coming to dance class if she did. I bit my nails to the quick and sometimes they bled, just like Mom's. It's not easy to have manicured nails when you don't have any, and between riding horses, picking stickers and working in the garden, my nails were a mess. After the first hour of instruction we were told to sit in our assigned seat and the music began.

"Gentlemen, please ask a lady to dance," the teacher said.

I waited for a boy to ask me to dance and Mom was right, there were boys in class taller than me. A boy approached, but he asked the short girl in the seat beside me to dance.

Another boy approached, but he asked the short girl on the other side of me to dance. Before long, all the tall boys were on the dance floor dancing with short girls. I was one of the last girls asked to dance and the boy was shorter than Dan.

"How did class go tonight, sweetie?" Mom asked, as I walked in the door.

"I'm not going back."

"I've paid for the classes and you're supposed to go every week for the next two months."

"I got my fingers hit with a ruler because I bite my nails, and the tall boys asked short girls to dance. I was the last girl asked to dance and the boy was shorter than Dan. And you forgot to tell me the rules, Mom!" I said, as I slammed my bedroom door.

"When you start something, you finish it," Dad said the next morning. "That's the way we do things, right? You can't quit."

"Dad, I know that's what you think and I know that's what you've taught us, but sometimes there are things I don't want to do."

138

"Sometimes in life we have to do things we don't want to. That's the way life is. Your Mom took the time to sign you up and pay for the classes. It's a good lesson to learn: you finish what you start."

I didn't stop biting my nails, but I brushed them with a nailbrush and put Vaseline on my hands and Mom polished my nails. Didn't matter, that teacher hit the tips of my fingers every class and it was humiliating. When it was time to ask someone to dance, I got up and asked the tallest, best-looking boy in class. One of the rules was that if you were asked to dance, you couldn't say no. As class went on, I learned it didn't matter how tall the boy was, it was how I felt about myself.

"Being tall is a gift and you'll figure that out," Dad said. He was right.

Donna and I took ballet and tap lessons. Donna used what she learned in ballet class to become one of the best gymnasts on the school gymnastics team.

Mom said dance classes would help with my coordination, posture and grace. Dad said I should concentrate on sports because I was athletic, strong and fast.

I decided sports was more my thing. Putting on a leotard, a tutu, ballet slippers and standing at a barre to make my body do things it wasn't built to do got old and boring. I was not the ballerina type and I had to face it.

After Mom picked Donna and me up from dance class on Fridays, we went to the local soda fountain for ice-cream and ordered whatever we wanted. Roseberry's Soda Fountain was an old-fashioned drug store with a long, narrow soda fountain on one side of the store. Mrs. Roseberry made the best chocolate sundaes and banana splits, Joe and Dan's favorites.

"I want everything on mine, lots of everything. Can I have two cherries?" Joe asked.

"That will cost you double," Mrs. Roseberry said with a smile. "I've never seen two boys eat a chocolate sundae and a banana split so fast. I'm surprised you don't have an ice-cream headache."

"What's an ice-cream headache?" Joe asked.

"I guess if you have to ask, you've never had one," she said, laughing.

We sat at the soda counter on black, chrome stools that spun 360 degrees. Friday afternoons the soda shop was the hangout for the high school kids before the football game, the girls arriving in their cheerleading uniforms and the boys in their school sweaters. I couldn't wait to go to high school and be one of the grown-up kids.

"Your Dad and I came here after school on Fridays when we were in high school. Your Dad was handsome in his school sweater with his letters and medals," Mom said. "His senior year, your Dad's sweater was heavy, covered with all his awards, and I loved wearing it."

Most of the boys in high school played on the football, basketball, baseball and track teams, like my Dad. There wasn't much to do in Winters after school except play sports, as even the movie theater closed. The nearest town was Davis, where the University of California was located, twenty minutes away.

Construction of the Monticello Dam at Lake Berryessa brought jobs and people to Winters. The BLM office opened in the 1950s and closed about ten years later when the dam was finished. All of us kids were fascinated by the Glory Hole, a cement, funnel-shaped spillway 70 feet in diameter, which allowed water to bypass the dam when the water level in the lake reached capacity. As the lake filled, the water spilled into the Glory Hole and Dad drove us to the dam so we could see it.

"Dad, is it true that a man went down the Glory Hole in a barrel and survived?" Joe asked.

"Who told you that?" Dad said, as we stood above the dam at the lookout.

"You did," I said.

"Well then, it must be true. Once the water spills into the Glory Hole, it falls 200 feet before coming out at the bottom of the dam."

"Dad, no one could live through that; you must have made it up," I said.

Dad was a good storyteller and we couldn't tell if he was pulling our leg, telling the truth or exaggerating. It didn't matter; we believed everything Dad said, most of the time.

Dad loved to horse around and he'd say the craziest things to us kids: "Turn off the lights, were you born in a barn?" or "She's as ugly as a mud fence," or "He's as slow as smoke off manure." He was always teasing us and pulling pranks on us and made a competition out of everything. Footraces were one of his favorites.

"On your marks. Get set. Go!" Dad said, as he dropped his hand from above his head.

We sprinted to the oak tree 200 yards up the dirt road from our house toward the fields. We never wore shoes and Dad always gave the boys a head start. It was only fair, he said, because they were little and he didn't want them to lose every time. Dad ran backwards and beat us, but as I grew up I gave Dad a run for his money, and by the time I finished high school I could beat him, on a good day. I could beat Rick, Charlie, Ruth and Bruce too.

Dad was known for his knee-slap game and we all knew the outcome, but played along anyway, even though we lost. Dad sat next to one of us or next to one of his nieces and nephews, and out of the blue the game would begin.

"If this was your knee," he said, as he slapped his knee, "and this was my knee," he said, as he slapped your knee, "I'd hit your knee this hard," he said, as he slapped his knee harder, "and my knee that hard," he said, as he slapped your knee with all his might.

It was a running joke around the house as we waited for the next unknowing relative or guest to sit next to Dad at a party or family gathering. It got so no one wanted to sit by him.

I didn't realize how protected we were being together as one big family so much of the time. Mom and Dad led us to believe that the world off the farm was like our world on the farm, but it wasn't. I know that's why Mom always told us, "Treat others as you want to be treated. Love your neighbor as yourself. Show people kindness. Tell the truth." That's how Mom lived her life. Living my life by those beliefs was tested more than once as I grew up.

Down the lane from our house was a labor camp owned by our neighbors, the Marianis, and their farm laborers lived in the camp. The Marianis' orchards sat alongside Grandpa's property and every morning I walked by the labor camp to catch the school bus. One of the boys who lived in the camp was in my eighth-grade class. David was nice and good-looking and I liked him until he started spreading hurtful lies.

"Here comes the tramp from the farm," the boys said, during recess. "We didn't know a good girl like you put out for boys in the camp."

"What are you talking about?"

"David told us. Your secret is out."

"What secret? What did David tell you?"

"That you did it with him in the orchard."

"Did what?"

"Come on, you know. You did it with him in the orchard."

"Did what with him? I don't know what you're talking about."

"David told everyone that you did it with him."

"You mean, I had sex with him?"

"Yeah, you screwed him. What do you think we mean?"

"That's not true. I never did it with David. He's my friend, but I never had sex with him."

"He told us all about it."

142

"It didn't happen. I would never do that."

I couldn't believe David said those ugly things. I wouldn't make up lies about him and I hated him for saying bad things about me. I wouldn't sit by him on the bus and I didn't look at him or talk to him.

"Mom, I don't feel good. I'm staying home from school today."

"Come here and let me take a look at you," said Mom, as she put her hand on my forehead. "You don't have a fever and you look fine to me. Is there something you're not telling me? Did something happen at school?"

I burst into tears. "David told everyone in class that I, that we..."

"That you what?" I didn't want to tell Mom what the kids were saying about me.

"That I did it with him. That I had sex with him in the orchard," I said, with tears in my eyes. "He told Johnny."

"Are you sure he said that?"

"All the kids in school are talking about it."

"You know the kids in your class are not going to believe him, and not Johnny. Get dressed, I'll drive you to school," said Mom, as she put her arms around me. "You ignore David and don't speak to him. You've done nothing to be ashamed of, remember that. I'll call the principal."

"No Mom, you can't call the principal. The kids will find out and it will only make things worse. Promise you won't do anything."

Mom raised us with her quiet strength and unwavering faith, but if anyone did something that hurt one of us she came to our defense like a lioness protecting her cubs. Harvest ended in a couple of weeks and David's father went to work at another farm. David and his family moved away and I never saw him again. I realized then that people did mean and hurtful things to one another for no reason, but that's not how I was raised.

"I never believed what David told me about you," Johnny said. "Heck, you won't even kiss me and you've been my girlfriend for two years."

Johnny got his first kiss right then and there on the school grounds. I had no idea how to kiss and Johnny didn't either. After graduation, Johnny's Dad took a job in southern California and Johnny moved away and I was heartbroken. Mom threw a going away party for his family and one of our teachers played the guitar and I almost died when my teacher started to sing.

> *Tears will fall just like rain,*
> *a wooly bully, a wooly bully.*
> *Cause Johnny is leaving without Lorraine,*
> *a wooly bully, a wooly bully, a wooly bully.*

What did I know about love at 13?

Along with my siblings and cousins, we spent the summer like always, working on the farm and swimming on the swim team. There were only four girls in my age group and our relay team was the best in the league. No one could beat Niki, Liz, Joy and me.

That summer Dad taught me to drive the Ford tractor and the New Holland hay swather, and I cultivated sugar beets and cut alfalfa, and saved every penny to buy a new car in three years when I would turn 16. I drove the grain truck, hauling barley and wheat from the fields to the grain silos, and I didn't need a driver's license because all the roads were on Grandpa's property.

Dad grew grain on the rolling hills several miles from our house on the back acres of the farm. He and Ron drove the grain harvesters and Donna drove the bank out wagon, a monstrous piece of machinery with an open cab and a six-ton, V-shaped bin. The bank out wagon sat five feet off the ground on gigantic rubber tires, four feet in diameter, and hauled the grain out of the field to trucks sitting at the bottom of the hill in the flats. The trucks transported the grain to silos where it was stored before being sold.

"Bank out" is a term farmers used long ago that meant nothing more than to move the grain out of the field. In the old days, grain was harvested with a thrasher attached to a side header on wheels pulled by 32 mules and dumped into 125-pound sacks that were sewn closed, laid in the field and hauled out on mule-drawn wagons. Grain harvest took all summer back then because Grandpa grew more acres of grain, plus harvesters weren't motorized yet, and the mules had to rest several times during the day and be watered and fed. Dad worked in harvest all summer when he was a kid and drove the grain trucks when he was 13. When Dad was a senior in high school he operated a side hill harvester, which at that time was pulled by a Caterpillar D-2 tractor that his cousin drove. When harvest was over, Dad spent the rest of the summer cutting star thistle, cockle burrs, horehound weeds and any other weeds that would harm the sheep that Grandpa's brother grazed in the hills.

By the time all of us kids worked in harvest, the grain harvester was motorized. Donna would drive the bank out wagon under the harvester's auger as Dad dumped the grain from the harvester into the bin on the bank out wagon. The hills were steep and the bank out wagon often slid down the hill. Dad wouldn't stop the harvester to unload; he said it was a waste of time. If Donna couldn't keep the bank out wagon in line with the harvester, the grain dumped on her head and the chaff from the barley covered her in a layer of fine, itchy dust that stuck to her sweaty skin like glue. She didn't complain, much.

"What are you doing?" Dad yelled, as he opened the harvester door and motioned Donna to move forward. "Speed up, you're driving too slow."

"The back tires are slipping down the hill and it's too steep to unload. Stop the stupid harvester," Donna yelled, motioning with her arms.

Donna ate chaff and barley all summer and she and Dad were constantly hollering at one another, Donna wanting him to slow down and Dad wanting her to keep up. I was glad I didn't have to drive the bank out wagon. I drove the four-ton, 1950 Chevrolet, flatbed dump trucks with hydraulic lifts that held 12 tons of grain, and waited for Donna to come off the hill and unload while I lay in the sun in my cutoffs and tank top, listening to my transistor radio. That burned my sister up; she didn't get breaks. She'd bomb down the hill with a full load, dump the grain in the truck and I'd race to the silos. When my cousin Ruth was old enough, she drove the barley trucks too, but I'd had a couple of years of practice and was a lot faster than she was most of the time.

"What took you so long?" Dad asked, when I returned late after dumping a load one afternoon. He was standing on the ground next to the harvester parked at the bottom of the hill. "The bin on the harvester is full and the bin on the bank out wagon is full. We're gonna be behind the rest of the day."

"I couldn't get the auger motor started, Dad. I pulled and pulled on the rope, but it wouldn't turn over."

"Next time, get the mechanic from the shop to help you."

"I did and he couldn't get it started either. He gave the motor too much choke and it flooded."

Dad threw his hands in the air and climbed up on the harvester. I knew what he was thinking. *Do I have to do everything around here myself?*

Unloading took thirty minutes, on a good day. I backed the truck over an eight-foot metal trough with an auger in the bottom. The auger's steel, rotating circular blade moved the grain through a narrow shaft from the trough to the top of the grain silo. I started the auger motor using a rope crank and sometimes the motor started on the first few cranks. But lots of times I had to yank it over and over, and I cussed that damn rope. All Dad had to do was buy a new auger motor, but no, we could make do one more summer with the old crank motor, he was sure of that. When the motor started, I opened the tailgate on the truck and the grain fell into the trough. If things went according to plan, I was back in the field in under an hour, but some days things didn't go according to plan.

Dad told me the story of his friend's son who stood on the back of the dump truck to see how much grain was left to be unloaded, slipped, and fell into the trough and lost his leg. Dad was always telling us how to do things his way. He'd been working on the farm since he was six years old and had never been seriously injured. He thought about what he did before he did it and knew what would happen if he was careless. Besides, Dad had a great deal of respect for his work and didn't take anything for granted, but some of the equipment was just plain old and I didn't think as quick on my feet as he did.

The grainfields were dry and brittle and the old harvester overheated and sparks flew into the stubble. I was the one to race home in the truck when accidents happened.

"Mom, Mom, call the fire department!" I screamed, as I burst through the front door. "The harvester started a fire in the grainfield. Hurry Mom, the wind's blowing and the grain will burn up."

"Fire in the hills four miles north of Winters. Load out in one minute." Mom overheard the announcement as she was on the phone reporting the fire. "It's the Romingers. They must be harvesting again."

Before Dad could afford to buy modern harvesters, most summers a grain fire started in the field and we were lucky the fire burnt the stubble and not the grain. Fire trucks were in the field in minutes and we'd jump on the back of the truck with the firemen. The fire was frightening, but the ride was thrilling, and when the fire was out, the firemen stopped by the house for a cold drink. It was the talk of the town for a day or two. Most of the firemen were volunteers and sat next to us in church and all of us kids went to the same school. Some of the firemen hunted with Dad and he was on the Fire Commission, but the only thing our friends wanted to know was what it was like to ride on the fire truck.

Working for Dad had its advantages. If something important came up he let us leave work early. We didn't have to worry about getting fired if we screwed up. If it was hot and miserable in the fields, we got to cut out of work and ski in the canal. But Dad never let us forget that summertime was about harvest.

"Get up, time's a wastin.' There's work to do," Dad said every morning.

By 6 a.m., Dad had been to the shop, started the workers in the fields and fueled the equipment. Our day started at sunrise and ended at sundown. Dad expected a lot from us and wanted us to do things his way. By the time we were teenagers, all of us kids worked on the farm all summer. Dad insisted on it. That was just fine with me, as I was saving my money to buy a car.

Dad wanted us to learn how to do most everything on the farm, but some jobs were not as easy as he made them look.

"Being a good irrigator is an art," Dad said, as we walked on the ditch bank at the end of the field.

"What do you mean by that?" I asked.

"Once the water starts down the furrow, you have to work around the clock. If the soil gets too wet, it cuts off the oxygen to the roots and the plant will die. Not all fields are irrigated the same, it depends on the type of soil and the crop that's planted. The water can't stand in the furrow so you add more siphons if the water isn't moving fast enough. In some fields, we only irrigate every other furrow."

"I guess there's more to it than I thought."

"A good irrigator knows the field and he knows the soil."

"Can you teach me how to start a siphon?"

"Siphons are made of aluminum and come in several lengths and diameters. They transfer water out of the ditch at the end of the field into the furrow. You have to submerge one end of the siphon in the ditch water like this and cover the other end with the palm of your hand. Move the siphon back and forth fast with your palm tight on the end and you'll create atmospheric pressure that draws the water into the siphon. When enough pressure builds up and you feel the water against your palm, lay the siphon over the bank like this. The pressure will force the water through the pipe and into the furrow," Dad said. "See?"

"This isn't easy," I said, as I tried to start the siphon.

Dad walked down the ditch bank, starting a siphon every fifteen seconds. It took me a lot longer and I was soaking wet. There was definitely a knack to being an irrigator.

"I think we should leave the irrigating to the irrigators. You don't want to be in the field at night in the dark all alone."

I had to admit Dad was right. Irrigating was a big responsibility and I didn't want to drown any of his crops. Dad's livelihood depended on the earth and Dad was one with the earth—firm, fair and faithful. Like we always said, Dad had dirt in his veins, not blood.

Every summer, the Rominger Family Picnic was held at Winters City Park and 100 of our relatives drove miles and miles from across the state to attend the potluck picnic held the first Sunday of June. After lunch, we played baseball and everyone played, from 2 years old to 80. Grandpa pitched and no one argued. Dad looked forward to the picnic all summer and loved sitting around, shooting the bull as he called it, with all his relatives, some that he only saw once a year. One of my favorite photos is a picture of Donna and Mom and Dad and me sitting on the grass at the family picnic in 1954. Mom is sitting next to Dad and his legs are crossed and he's holding Donna on one knee and me on the other. Mom has on a white blouse and a flowered skirt, and Dad has his Levis rolled up and his white shirt unbuttoned. Dad's hands are supporting Donna and me on his knees and his hands are almost as big as our heads.

The summer before I started high school in 1965, Mom took Donna and me to the Cow Palace in San Francisco to see The Beatles. We talked about it all summer, and I remember telling every one of my cousins at the family picnic that Donna and I were going to see our favorite band. The Beatles were the biggest thing to hit America and every girl I knew was in love with Paul, but I was in love with George. I wore a black-and-white print skirt and a black blouse with black lace stockings. We begged Mom to drop us off early so we could stand outside the venue and try to get a peek of The Beatles when they arrived in their limo. Everyone went crazy when they arrived and the air filled with the screams of thousands of girls. I remember Donna and I picked up sand off the ground where their limo had driven and put it in a Kleenex! Once the concert started, the screeching inside the arena was so loud we couldn't hear them sing and I just wanted everyone to shut up. Donna and I had great seats close to the front, but people crowded the stage and we were forced to stand on our chairs the whole concert so we could see and keep ourselves from being pushed and shoved. It was total pandemonium. I thought The Beatles were divine, but girls made fools out of themselves, crying and carrying on like they'd never seen good-looking boys who could sing and play instruments at the same time. Donna and I had watched The Beatles the first time they appeared on the *The Ed Sullivan Show* in 1964, and Mom promised us if they went on tour and performed close to where we lived, she would do her best to buy tickets. She kept her promise.

We listened to music at home all the time and watched the *The Ed Sullivan Show* and *The Lawrence Welk Show*. Mom had a great voice and loved to sing along with The Lennon Sisters and The Everly Brothers, songs like "Wake Up Little Susie" and "All I Have to Do Is Dream." We had a record player and collected 45s, and our favorite groups were Frankie Valli and The Four Seasons, The Dave Clark Five, Herman's Hermits and The Monkeys. Mom used to always say that if she hadn't got married she would have been a singer. She sang every Sunday in the church choir and she was without a doubt the best singer in town.

Mom also loved movies, *Singing in the Rain* with Ginger Rogers and Fred Astaire and *It's a Wonderful Life* with James Stewart and Donna Reed. I swear Mom must have seen them 25 times. Also Audrey Hepburn, one of Mom's favorites, in *My Fair Lady* and *Breakfast at Tiffany's*. My favorites were all the Shirley Temple movies and Tarzan movies with Johnny Weissmuller; no one swung through the jungle, beat his chest or had a louder Tarzan yell. And we had our favorite television shows: *Father Knows Best, Leave it to Beaver, I Love Lucy, Gilligan's Island, The Beverly Hillbillies, Gunsmoke* and *Bonanza. Bonanza* was my favorite by far; I loved Little Joe and Hoss, and their family's life revolved around their ranch, the Ponderosa, just like my family's life revolved around the farm. My brothers liked *The Flintstones* and *The Jetsons*, but I would rather ride horses across wide open plains than live in the Stone Age in Bedrock with Fred and Wilma.

Winters High School cheerleading squad, 1968

Chapter 14

In 1965, I entered Winters High School, the same high school my parents had graduated from 18 years before.

I remember what I wore my first day: a short, straight plaid skirt and gold blouse with red leather lace-up heels. Mom helped me pick the outfit. She was the prettiest Mom of all my friends and the best dressed.

There were 275 students in school and 70 kids in my freshman class. I got up early to make sure I could wash the breakfast dishes, fix my hair and walk to the end of the lane in time to catch the bus. Mom made Donna and me do the dishes every morning before we went to school. When my Dad started high school, they didn't have school buses, so at 14 he got his driver's license and drove to school. Taking the bus was a lot better than riding my bike.

"Not mush again," I said. "Can't we have something different for breakfast once in a while?"

"It's not mush. It's oatmeal," Mom said.

"It's mush," I said, as I put my full dish in the kitchen sink. "It sticks to the pot and I have to soak it before I can get it clean. I'm not hungry anyway and I'm too excited and nervous. I'll be done with these dishes in five minutes and then I'm leaving for the bus."

"How about I drive you to school your first day?"

"Great, Mom. Now I have time to fix my hair."

Living in a small town with a mother and father who grew up there was a blessing and a curse. We knew everyone and Mom was on the school board so I knew I couldn't get away with much.

I loved sports. Dad was a big jock and both my brothers and sister were athletic and coordinated. We were constantly playing games on the farm and I couldn't wait to join every girls team and go to practice after school.

"Ref, are you blind?" Dad yelled from the stands. "Stay on her. Shoot the ball. Get out of the key."

Knowing Dad was in the bleachers gave me confidence. He left work to come watch me play, and even though Mom said the farm came first, I knew better. Dad worked long hours so we could have the things we wanted, but he never missed my games, and even though I played for a small school, we had a championship team in one sport every year. Dad pushed me to excel and I'm glad he did. He helped me become a better athlete and believed in me, a faith that changed me and shaped me whether I wanted to admit it or not. After a basketball game or a track meet, we came home and he showed me how to do things better.

"When those tall girls get in front of you under the basket, step with your opposite foot in front of them like this and don't be afraid of them. If they push you, push them back. If the guard passes you the ball high, don't bring the ball down in front of you before you shoot. It gives the short guards a chance to stop you. Shoot it from high like this."

"I can't do that every time, Dad."

"Yes you can. You can do anything you set your mind to and don't let anyone ever tell you different. Think about what you're doing every minute and don't take your eye off the ball. You can do this. You're a much better player than you think you are."

Track started after basketball and I trained by running along the fields up to the yellow house. There were miles of dirt roads on the farm as far as you could see. I'd take off, and before long I'd hear Dad's pickup behind me.

"Pick up the pace, you're poking it," Dad yelled. "You can't win the 440 training like that."

"Give me a break, Dad," I yelled back.

"No excuses, get going," he hollered, as he drove beside me and honked the horn.

I trained for months to compete in the Youth Day track meet. Youth Day was a longstanding tradition at Winters High School, held the last Saturday of April, the day the high school kids took over the town. Students worked all year on the events for Youth Day that began with a breakfast, followed by a parade, barbecue, baseball game, regional track meet, children's carnival, talent show and dinner dance.

All of us kids walked in the Youth Day Parade every year while growing up, starting from when we were in grammar school, pulling our red wagons with our dogs in them, bandannas around their necks, or riding our tricycles and bicycles. We'd dress up in farm clothes or cowboy costumes and wave at everyone sitting along the streets on their chairs and on the curb. Thank goodness we marched before the horses so we didn't have to worry about the horse poop. Mom used to walk alongside us on the street just in case.

Everyone in Winters turned out for the big day, and the money raised was used for after-school programs. A senior was elected chairman and selected a committee to plan and organize the day; being chairman of Youth Day was an honor and a hell of a lot of work. The Lion's Club, The Chamber of Commerce, The Knights of Columbus, The Rotary, every civic organization in town participated. Each class had a float in the parade, as did most businesses, and bands came from local high schools in the county to march in the parade along with dance troupes, horse groups, antique car clubs and fire departments. Each class elected a Youth Day Princess and the senior class elected the Youth Day Sweetheart to ride on the senior float.

"Mom, Dad. You're not going to believe what happened today," I screamed with excitement as I ran in the back door after school. "I got elected Youth Day Princess for the freshman class and I get to ride on the senior float with the Youth Day Sweetheart. I can't believe my class picked me."

"I can," Mom said. "I'm proud of you. Did you know Youth Day started when your father and I were in high school? It's a tradition that has carried on all these years."

People came from throughout the county to compete in the talent show to win the first, second and third place cash prizes, and the show was a serious competition. A stage was built on the grass quad between the high school and the gymnasium and we sold hundreds of tickets. The long gown I wore as Youth Day Princess was hideous and went to the Goodwill, but I kept the pearl pendant necklace the princesses received as a gift.

I played wing on the girls' field hockey team. It was a game of stamina and skill, and even though I wasn't the best with the hockey stick, when I got the ball and took off down the field no one could catch me. Running races on the farm with my cousins and brothers and sister paid off.

Donna was a good athlete. She was graceful and limber and I wasn't, so she competed on the gymnastics team and I didn't. We played the same sports, but didn't compete against each other; we were two years apart and she played junior varsity when I played varsity. Good thing I didn't have to compete against my sister. When school was out, we swam on the swim team in different age groups.

"Go Donna. Go Donna," I yelled. "Go...Go...Go."

Donna was swimming butterfly at the championship meet in Davis and the race was neck and neck. The lifeguard added chlorine to the pool earlier in the day and the water was like milk. I was screaming and watching my parents in the bleachers cheer Donna on when I looked to see the finish as she raised her head out of the water to take a breath and smashed into the concrete wall. Her arms went limp as she sank under the water. I turned to see my father scrambling through parents, jumping off the bleachers and racing to the end of the pool.

"Donna, grab my arms," Dad said.

She didn't even cry. I swear my sister was tougher than a boiled owl.

"I can get out by myself," Donna said. She was stubborn and would never admit anything hurt her. But after a long silence, she reached her arms out toward Dad.

Her two front teeth had split in half and it wasn't long before she had caps on her teeth.

I started my sophomore year as a song leader. During tryouts at the end of my freshman year I was nervous and sick to my stomach. The student body elected only six girls and I was one of them. As a child, I remember going to the football games with Dad, watching the pompom girls and dreaming of being one when I grew up. Mrs. Bruhn was the only seamstress in town and made the outfits for the cheerleaders and song leaders. Our school colors were red and white and our mascot was an Indian warrior; we were the Winters Warriors. During the games we performed on the red-clay dirt track that surrounded the football field, so you can imagine what our white outfits looked like at the end of the game.

"When you came home and told me your song leader outfits for football were made of white wool, I should have put my foot down," Mom said. "Do you have any idea how much I spent on dry cleaning this season?"

"We plan to have red wool outfits for basketball, but maybe we should have white ones. It will be much easier to keep them clean since we're in the gym for the games."

"Red outfits sound good to me," Mom said, "unless you plan to pay the dry cleaning bill."

We chose red outfits for basketball. My Mom wasn't the only mother to put her foot down.

The gymnasium had been built when Dad was in high school and there wasn't another gym like it in the county. It resembled a gigantic, white wooden shoebox with red letters on the front that spelled GYMNASIUM. Dad was the star of the basketball team when he was in high school and I could picture him running down the court, dunking the ball and looking up in the stands at Mom, one of the cheerleaders, while the crowd screamed. I imagined a packed gym and not an empty seat in the place. My Dad was a pretty good athlete considering he never touched a basketball until he got to high school; they didn't have any basketballs at Union School.

Inside the gym, raised wooden bleachers sat 10 feet above the basketball court, and as people entered through the double wooden doors in front, the gym floor was straight ahead. Rows and rows of elevated bleachers ran the length of the court, accessible only by climbing the wooden stairs on both ends of the gym floor. Spectators had a full view of the court no matter where they sat. It was a great gym, but it was falling down and needed major repairs. It was bulldozed and we got a new gym my sophomore year. Some things can't be replaced. The gym was a landmark and Dad and I agreed it was a shame to tear it down.

After basketball season ended, I put away my pompoms and put on my track shoes. At the championship meet I got my butt kicked by a tall redhead from Rio Vista, one of the high schools in our conference. Coming around the final turn in the 440 I was in the lead and she came up beside me and blew past me.

"You did your best," Dad said, as he put his arms around me. He was as disappointed as I was.

Dad taught us to do our best, and sometimes our best didn't mean we were first. I wouldn't forget how I felt seeing that redhead's ass cross the finish line in front of me.

That summer I turned 16 and wanted to have a slumber party and invite all my girlfriends and the song leaders. Mom agreed.

"My Mom said I could come. How do I get to your house?" Kate asked.

"Take Road 89 out of town towards Madison. It's four miles to Road 29A, and make a left. My house is at the end of the lane."

"See you Friday night. Can't wait," Kate said, as she hung up the phone.

"Fifteen girls! I better make sure I have enough food," Mom said. "We'll have a barbecue on Friday night and you can sleep on the lawn under the birch tree. It will be cooler outside in the evening."

"Mom, some of the girls won't sleep outside on the grass in sleeping bags."

"Well then, they can sleep on the floor in the living room." After the girls arrived we went swimming and floated on inner tubes in the canal.

"Come on, get in," I said, as they stood on the ditch bank.

"I'm not a very good swimmer and I don't swim in irrigation ditches. They're dirty and my Mom says bugs and snakes live in irrigation ditches," Patty said.

"It's not dirty, it's just muddy, and there aren't any snakes in the water. Better be careful though because there might be snakes in the grass where you're standing," I said.

"Oh, my God," Patty screamed.

"I'm only kidding. You don't have to swim if you don't want to."

The girls asked if they could ride my horse, so I put the saddle on Lady. I wanted my friends to have fun and love the farm like I did, but most of my friends had never ridden a horse and my horse was not easy to control. The riding didn't last long.

"Get me down. She won't do what I want her to do," Susan said.

"I told you not to let go of the reins. You have to hold them tight."

I'd never seen such a bunch of babies in my life. Of course, being raised on a farm is different than being raised in town, but I wasn't afraid to try new things and never freaked out about getting dirty or bugs crawling on me.

Dad barbecued hot dogs and hamburgers and after we ate we went for a walk up the dirt road toward the fields. Before long, a few farmworkers from the camp drove up in their beat-up white pickup.

"Hey, *mamacitas*. What are you doing out here all alone? Want some company? Would you like to take a ride?" the boys yelled. "Come and have a beer with us?"

When we didn't answer them, they began yelling dirty things in Spanish.

"I'm not going to listen to this, I'm going back to your house," Maria said.

"Ignore them. Let's get off the road and walk in the field and they'll go away. They're drinking like they do every night about this time," I said.

Jane picked up a rotten honeydew melon in the field and threw it at the pickup.

"Get out of here and leave us alone," she screamed, as she hit the bumper with the rotten melon.

"You're trespassing on my father's property," I yelled, as they sped away in the pickup. "Let's go back to the house."

We were sitting on the lawn when the workers in the pickup pulled up to the back door.

"Shit," I said, to the girls. "What are they doing here?"

"Lorraine, come here," Dad yelled. "The boys said you threw a melon at their pickup and cracked the windshield."

"The melon didn't hit the windshield, it hit the bumper and the melon was rotten. They were following us on the road yelling vulgar words and calling us names, and they asked us to get in the truck and have a beer. Look at the pickup, Dad. There's not a side without a dent or scratch and every window has a crack in it," I said.

"She's right, Mr. Rominger," Maria said. "They were calling us names and saying nasty things in Spanish and I bet they didn't know I speak Spanish. Would you like me to tell you what they called us?"

160

"That won't be necessary. I'll take care of this. You girls stay around the house."

I couldn't hear everything Dad said to them, but the workers drove off. I overheard something about trespassing, offering beer to minors and calling the sheriff. None of them had a green card and the sheriff was the last person they'd want to talk to.

Dad apologized for questioning me and said the workers probably thought they could get some money out of him. "I should have told them to leave the minute they drove up."

"Dad, we're not little girls anymore. We're growing up in case you haven't noticed and the workers were hitting on us."

Dad didn't want to hear that.

We slept outside in sleeping bags under the bright stars and I woke up in the middle of the night to two of my girlfriends screaming at each other.

"I never said that," Sandra said.

"You did too. Half the girls in class told me you were going around school saying things about me. You're a liar. You think all the boys like you, but they laugh behind your back and say terrible things about you," Kate said.

"Shut up. I'm not going to listen to this shit," Sandra yelled, as she climbed out of her sleeping bag.

"Don't scream at me. You're the one that started this," Kate yelled as she got out of her bag.

Sandra pushed Kate and Kate swung at Sandra.

"Stop fighting. You're going to wake my parents. What is the matter with the two of you?" I said, as I stood between them.

"This was a bad idea. I can't stand her and either she leaves or I leave," Sandra said.

"Neither one of you is leaving," I said.

"I mean it. Either she leaves or I leave," Sandra said, again.

"I don't want either one of you to leave," I said.

"Well, I can tell when I'm not wanted. She doesn't have to leave, I am," Sandra said.

Sandra picked up her stuff and headed to her car. "Sandra, don't leave. It's the middle of the night and you and Kate are my friends. I want you both to stay."

"Don't worry about me, I can take care of myself. Have a nice night...with all your goody girlfriends," Sandra said, as she drove away.

"How can you be friends with a girl like that? Her father and mother are nuts and she's insane," Kate said.

"She's unhappy and lonely. Her parents are never home and she doesn't have many friends and I feel sorry for her," I said.

"Well, I think she's a nutcase. Why do you hang out with her? She's talked trash about me over and over and none of it's true," Kate said.

We tried to sleep, but most of us sat up talking about Sandra and boys. Sandra tried too hard to be accepted. Speeding around in her fancy car in the parking lot, showing off in front of the guys, inviting the girls to her house with her closet full of clothes, her dresser covered with makeup and expensive perfumes. That was Sandra—she had everything she wanted and nothing she needed.

In the morning Mom cooked bacon and eggs and the girls didn't say much.

"You girls must have stayed up all night talking," Mom said. "Did you all agree your song-leading outfits are going to be red next year?"

We were sitting at the kitchen table. No one answered. Finally I said, "Mom, we didn't talk about that."

One by one the girls left and went home.

"I noticed Sandra wasn't at breakfast. Did she have to leave early?"

"Mom, last night Sandra and Kate got into a screaming match and a fight started. Sandra went home in the middle of the night and created a scene. I didn't know what to do. The other girls were glad she left."

"Maybe you should call Sandra and make sure she got home? It would be a nice thing to do. I know you and Kate have been friends for years so why don't you call her too? The girls told me what a nice time they had when they left, so don't let it ruin your party."

It was my fault. I knew they didn't get along, but I didn't think Sandra and Kate would make a scene in front of the other girls. Things were changing, we were all growing up and not everything was permanent. Even the gym had been torn down. How could I know what would last?

Edsel station wagon, 1958

Chapter 15

I drove a 1958 Edsel station wagon my junior year.

One of the farmworkers couldn't afford to pay back his advance and owed Dad money when he quit. Dad inherited a white Edsel station wagon with red interior. This was not my dream car, but I got my driver's license during the summer and Dad told me the Edsel was mine. It was a heck of a lot better than riding the bus. I had saved money for years to buy a new car when I turned 16, but Dad decided I had to wait until I graduated from high school to buy my own car. He wanted to make sure I was a good driver, so until then I was stuck with Old Ed.

Donna didn't attend Winters High her freshman year when I was a junior. She was too smart for her own britches according to her homeroom grammar school teacher, and she acted up, not because she was a bad kid, but because it was impossible to keep her interested in her studies. She was bored to death in eighth grade, picked fights, misbehaved in class, talked too much and was just plain irritating, so Mom and Dad sent Donna to Ursuline, a Catholic girls high school in Santa Rosa, a two-hour drive from Winters. I missed having her around.

I'll admit I was embarrassed to drive the old beat-up Edsel into the parking lot at high school after dropping my brothers and cousins at grammar school. It never failed, the senior boys would be hanging out by their brand-new cars until the bell rang for first period.

"Hey, Rominger," the boys yelled. "What junkyard did you steal the Edsel from?" as they laughed at me.

My saving grace was that the Edsel became a moving billboard and pep rally car on football game days. The cheer squad spent hours painting signs on white butcher paper that we hung in the hallways and the gym. We painted on the side of the car in big red letters, "Go Warriors – Beat Rio Vista," or whatever team we were playing. The cheer squad cruised around town with me as I honked the horn, yelling cheers out the window. It wasn't long before the senior boys on the football team thought the Edsel was pretty cool; our school colors were red and white and Old Ed was a perfect match.

"Hey, Dad. Guess what happened today at school?"

"Is it good news or bad news? Give me the good news first."

"Look at the school newspaper," I said, as I handed it to him. "Old Ed got Car of the Week. Isn't that great? It's kind of become the school mascot."

The first day Dad told me I could drive the Edsel to school, I thought he was nuts. I didn't want to seem ungrateful or hurt his feelings, but now that it was cool, I didn't have to worry about dings or scratches, and painting cheers on the side of the car was a brilliant idea.

The teachers at Winters High took great interest in their students and I got along with all of them. My Spanish teacher was the oldest teacher in school and one of the nicest. She dressed to the nines every day and wore high heels with her long gray hair in a French twist. I had Spanish last period and I remember the semester I had straight A's on my report card. When I handed her my card to give me my grade, she looked up at me and smiled. I had a B+ in Spanish, but she gave me an A–.

"Don't tell, but I'm not going to put a B at the end of all those A's," she whispered.

I had to study long and hard to get A's and B's and almost died the semester I got a C in Chemistry. I didn't let that happen again. My Home Economics teacher was also my 4-H leader and she could explain how to do anything. On the other hand, I had the same math teacher all four years and never learned much about algebra, geometry or trigonometry; I'm not sure he understood much about math either, or maybe it was his inability to explain anything complicated.

I fell in love my junior year and had no idea what love was at 16, but I knew I didn't want to spend time with anyone but Jack—far too much time, according to Mom and Dad. Dad took me to the school dances and picked me up until they gave in and let me go on a date with Jack in his car. It was about time; I had outgrown Dad being my chauffeur.

It was a big deal when Jack gave me his class ring and Mom and Dad were not happy. I had an 11:30 p.m. curfew and was only allowed to go out with Jack on weekends. My girlfriend could go out any night of the week they wanted, but not me. My parents were strict. Too strict, I decided.

"Mom, can I go to town to the library tonight and study with my project group? We're writing a report for school and need to work on it together."

"It's a school night and you need to be home by 9 p.m. No later, understood?"

Mom was the one I went to first to ask permission. She wasn't as strict as Dad and let me do things Dad wouldn't, and I know they disagreed. Because Mom was on the school board she knew what kids did in high school. Dad's life was centered on the farm and he had no idea what kids were up to. It was black or white with Dad and no gray in-between; it was either right or wrong.

"I told you nine o'clock young lady and it's ten. The library closed at nine tonight. Where have you been?"

"How do you know the library closed early tonight?"

"When you weren't home by 9:30 p.m., I went to the library looking for you. I want to know where you've been."

"I can't believe you came to town looking for me. We went to Sue's house to finish the report since we didn't get done when the library closed."

"The next time you're going to be late, pick up the phone and call me. Do you understand? Look at me, you better understand or you will not be going anywhere during the week."

"Fine, Mom. Take it easy."

"Don't tell me to take it easy or you won't be going to town at all during the week."

"OK, OK," I said, as I closed my bedroom door.

Mom let me go to town on a school night and Dad didn't like the idea. He would have said no if it had been up to him. Mom didn't like me talking back to her, something I hadn't done before. *Better keep your mouth shut*, I thought to myself. If they knew I'd been cruising around with Jack, drinking beer and not at the library, that would be the end of my going to town during the week.

Jack was popular, had lots of friends and was good looking. He was a senior when I was a junior and we were inseparable that year, spending Friday and Saturday nights together and every day at school. His family invited me to Squaw Valley for the weekend and Jack was mad at me for refusing to ski the black-diamond trail with him. He skied off and left me and I took a nasty fall and ended up in the emergency room with a gash on my leg that needed stitches. Jack spent the afternoon looking for me on the slopes and was frantic by the time I got back to the cabin. Served him right.

Mom and Dad said we spent too much time together, but as long as they believed my lies and I didn't get caught, I could see Jack when I wanted. One thing I learned during the weekend at Tahoe, Jack had a temper and that frightened me. I was completely taken by surprise when he hit me. No one had ever hit me before and I didn't know what to do. Dad would never lay a hand on Mom and I figured it was my fault. I did something to upset Jack so I would be the one to fix things.

"You aren't going to wear heels with your dress to the junior prom, are you?"

"Of course I am."

"I want you to wear flats. They take pictures at the prom and I don't want you to be taller than me in the photo."

"Mom bought me a pair of heels to match my dress. What am I supposed to tell her?"

"I don't care what you tell her, but I don't want you to wear heels."

I didn't have any other shoes to wear and I was not about to tell Mom my boyfriend demanded I wear flats. She would think I was nuts to put up with that. Jack was uncomfortable and made me feel guilty for not doing what he wanted, and the evening was a nightmare.

"If you love me and care about me, you would have done what I told you to do," Jack said, as he hit me in the car after the prom.

"Stop it! I've done nothing wrong and even if I did, you have no right to treat me this way."

"If you would just do what I tell you to do, none of this would happen."

When the photos from the prom came in the mail, Mom asked, "Why are you slouched over? You're tall and beautiful and you always stand up nice and straight. You're not still embarrassed about being tall, are you?"

"No, but Jack is. He asked me to wear flats to the prom so I wouldn't be taller than him in the photos. He was mad all night and made me feel terrible for wearing the heels you bought me and we had a big argument."

"Sweetie, this is not the boy for you. He should be proud of you, not ashamed. I hate to see you spend all your time with him and I think his going away to college will be a good thing."

Mom was the voice of calm and reason. I wanted to tell her what Jack did, but I knew how disappointed she would be in me for putting up with his behavior. Plus, she'd tell Dad and Dad would never understand. All I had to do was what Jack wanted and everything would be fine, I told myself. Mom had told me more than once that women stand by their man, and that women are the ones who compromise and sacrifice more in a relationship.

Mom and Dad encouraged me to play sports and compete, more so Dad. I think they were glad it took time away from my being with Jack. The day of the championship track meet, I spotted the red-haired girl from Rio Vista who had kicked my ass the year before and I was afraid she'd do it again. I looked up and saw Dad in the stands; he was always there and never let me down. I wanted to win this race for him as much as for myself.

"Runners, check in at the starting line. Five minutes to the start of the girls 440-yard run."

"Run your race, Lorraine. Don't think about anything else, just run your race." I could hear Dad's words in my head. "It's a dash and you have to run as fast as you can the whole way. Leave a little at the end because you know she has a kick."

"Runners, on your mark...set," off went the gun.

I ran as fast as I could. I heard the crackling of gravel against the hard clay as the shoes on the girls behind me hit the track. I came to the final turn and heard screams from the stands and footsteps grew louder as the redhead from Rio Vista came up beside me.

Come on, I said to myself. *This is your race to win.* We ran side by side for 20 yards and then I sprinted to the finish and left her in the dust.

"You cleaned her clock. Great job," Dad said, as he put his arms around me at the finish line.

"Thanks Dad. I had to beat her after last year."

"There's a scout here from an AAU women's track team in Sacramento who wants to talk to you. He was here to watch the girl from Rio Vista and was surprised you beat her."

"I'm with the Will's Spikettes in Sacramento. How long have you been running track?" the scout asked.

"A couple of years."

"I'd like to see if you'd be interested in running for the Spikettes. We train in Sacramento every day. Why don't you and your Dad talk it over? Here's my card. Give me a call in a few days and we can discuss it in more detail."

"Did you hear that? He scouts for Will Stephens. Will's Spikettes is the best AAU women's track team in the area and he coaches Kathy Hammond. I think she holds the world indoor record for the 440."

"Dad, those girls train every day for hours and don't do anything except run track and homework. They practice in Sacramento, an hour away."

"Let's talk about it tomorrow. You should at least go meet with him and hear what he has to say."

So began my AAU track career. There would be no cheerleading parties, no dates and no horses, just track. I tried out and made the team, but the tryouts nearly killed me. These girls were in a class by themselves.

"Hey, I know you're new," one of the girls said the first week. "Let me give you a little advice. I've been on the team for two years. Don't try to win every heat or you're going to be so sore you won't be able to walk. If you win every sprint, he'll expect you to win every sprint the next day and if you don't he'll make you run extra laps. You're going to die out here so take it easy. Stay in the bunch with the rest of us. I'm not afraid of you kicking my ass, I'm just giving you a little friendly advice. New girls come here, make the team and try to win every heat. Three hours is a long time every afternoon and you'll be dragging your ass across the finish line by the end of practice. He'll say you're doggin' it and he'll work you to death. I know what I'm talking about."

Boy, did she. I ran with the pack, but I didn't want to be part of the pack. I wanted to be the best.

Dad got up every morning with me to train. When I was younger, I dreamed of being an Olympic athlete. I came from a family of jocks and there wasn't a sport I didn't play in school. Every kid has that dream if they excel in a sport, don't they? But how many girls does that happen to? Not many.

Working out every morning and driving to Sacramento after school for practice took its toll on both Mom and me. Mom had kids at home and waited for three hours while I practiced. I realized how lucky I was to have parents that would do anything for me. Donna and I loved sports and we both knew I would have to train every day if I wanted to do well.

"Do you like the girls on the team?" Donna asked.

"Sure I do, but they are much better than me. Some of the girls have been running track on the team for years and I'm not sure I'll ever be good enough to compete with them. Practice is tough and I'm sore as hell every night. Plus, it's hard on Mom."

"Well, you have your driver's license and could drive yourself to Sacramento."

"Mom and Dad won't let me. Mom says it's too far and too much for me to do by myself. I'm going to Sacramento three days a week from now on and train here three days a week."

"Are you sure this is what you want to do?"

"All those girls do is run track and do homework. They don't date. They don't do anything. I haven't ridden my horse in weeks and I know if I quit Dad is going to be upset with me."

"You can't do this for Dad. You have to do it for yourself. Talk to Mom, she'll understand."

"I'm going to train every day for the next couple of months. We have a qualifying meet in Bakersfield and I'll be running against girls a lot faster than me. I'm going to wait and see how I do."

Dad overheard my conversation with Donna. "You have to want this more than anything, or it will never work. You have to believe that you have what it takes and that you can do it. You can't be the best in a couple of months, it will take years."

I got left in the dust at the qualifying meet and didn't even run against the best girls on the team. Dad thought I gave up. He said I had the talent and needed to be dedicated and train for years. But I didn't have it in me and quit. I couldn't give up everything for a chance at something that might never happen. Dad was disappointed.

"I think you should consider selling your horses," Dad said at dinner. "They need to be ridden. Your grandfather feeds them every morning and every night and it's not his responsibility."

"I haven't ridden my horses because I've been training."

"I think it's more than that. You've lost interest in your horses." I knew Dad thought I'd lost interest in everything except Jack. He thought I quit track so I could spend more time with Jack. Dad never came right out and said that, but I knew.

"I know my horses need to be ridden. I'm going on a trail ride this weekend."

I loved my horses, but Dad was right. I had neglected them and they were not my Grandpa's responsibility. Dad knew a farmer down the road who offered to buy my horses for his kids and I knew they'd have a good home.

Dad and I loaded Lady and Bay Boy into the horse trailer. I remembered riding with my girlfriends, jumping bales of hay and flying over Lady's head when she stopped dead in front of the bale. Or the day she fell over on me crossing the bridge, spooked by the fish splashing in the bottom of the ditch. She'd thrown me off more times than I could count and I had several broken bones to prove it. As I closed the trailer door, I saw Lady had gotten fat.

I cried all the way to their ranch. I didn't want to sell my horses, but it was the right thing to do. When we pulled into the barnyard the kids were standing there waiting and it reminded me of the day I was 10 and Dad and I brought Lady home. The kids had big smiles on their faces and I was relieved.

"What's her name? What's his name?" the girl asked.

"Her name is Lady and his name is Bay Boy."

"Don't worry. My brother and I will take good care of them," the girl said, as she took the ropes out of my hand. She looked like me at that age, tall with braids.

I put my arms around my horses' necks, rubbed their heads and gave them a hug. I said goodbye, goodbye to part of my childhood. As Dad and I drove away I looked in the side mirror and saw the girl and boy sitting on the horses and caught my smile in the mirror.

My gym teacher my senior year didn't like me and I didn't like her. She was the only teacher in Winters High School that I didn't get along with, even though I got all *A*'s in physical education all through high school and was first-string on every team. Maybe it was because she didn't have an athletic bone in her body and I was a good athlete. How she got a job teaching team sports I'll never know. She couldn't run down the court and bounce the basketball at the same time, and she was a terrible teacher and a worse coach. She didn't inspire or motivate or lead, all the things a coach needs to do. I didn't pay attention to her and shook my head and rolled my eyes every time she tried to show us a move on the court. I swear, she was afraid of the ball. She was uncoordinated, ran on her tiptoes and flirted with the senior boys; it was disgusting.

She had the last laugh. I ran for cheerleader and the girl with the most votes was named head cheerleader; it had always been that way at Winters High. At the pep rally, my gym teacher stood up in front of the student body and announced that Cathy had won head cheerleader. Two of my friends had counted the votes with the principal and told me I had received the most votes. When I went home and told Mom, she called the principal. Yes, he confessed, I did get the most votes and he was shocked that the gym teacher made such an announcement.

"Mom, that woman is a bitch. She's had it out for me since the first day of school. She didn't know what a fast break was and when I showed the girls on the team what do to, they made fun of her behind her back and she heard them. She hates me. How do you expect me to go to class and look her in the face? This is my last year of high school and I deserve to be head cheerleader. I won fair and square and she wrecked everything."

"What do you want the principal to do? Call Cathy and tell her and her parents that a mistake was made?"

"Then I'd go to school and everyone would call me a sore loser and feel sorry for Cathy. What about the gym teacher? What's going to happen to her?"

"The principal said she would be reprimanded."

"Then she'll be on my ass and bench me during the game."

"She won't do that. You're the best player on the team," Dad said.

"She thinks Allie is the best player. Allie's dad is a preacher and she can do no wrong as far as that bitch is concerned."

"You can make your point without using that kind of language," Dad said.

"I get screwed and you're worried about my language."

"You have to let this go. Life is not fair and you're going to have lots of disappointments. This won't be your last. Be the bigger person; you'll have other opportunities in life."

"Mom, you were head cheerleader your senior year at Winters High School. You know how much this means to me. This is so unfair."

"You're a cheerleader, that's what counts," Mom said. "I just don't know what we can do about this now."

"Bullshit. This is bullshit."

"Lorraine, do not use that kind of language. What have I taught you?" Dad said.

"You've taught me to stick up for myself, be tough and fight for what I know is right. That's what. Now I win, but I am supposed to suck it up and pretend like everything is OK. This is not my fault, but I'm the one who loses."

"No, you win by being the bigger person. No good deed goes unnoticed," Mom said.

"What a crock," I said.

I didn't have a choice. The announcement had been made and Cathy was head cheerleader. That was that.

Mom and Dad had no idea what was going on with Jack. Things got serious and out of control. I was in way over my head and lied to my parents every time Jack and I went out. The last thing I wanted was my parents finding out we were having sex in the back seat of Jack's car; they'd kill me. This was not the way my parents raised me.

Mom told me she and Dad didn't have sex until they got married and I didn't doubt what she said for a minute. Dad was the only man Mom had ever slept with and Mom was the only woman Dad had ever slept with. Mom and Dad believed marriage was a sacrament, a lifetime commitment, but I couldn't imagine marrying someone and not having sex before you married them. Most of the girls in my class were having sex and a couple of them had gotten pregnant. Rumors flew around town like leaves in a heavy storm and created quite a stir. My girlfriends and I confided in one another and I learned some of them used birth control. Mom would never hear of that and I knew I was playing with fire and freaked out every time my period was late. I came home with a hickey on my neck and couldn't walk around in a turtleneck, so I tried to hide it with makeup and that made it worse.

"Lorraine, what's that mark on your neck?" Mom asked.

"Just a bruise. I got hit in hockey practice."

"That doesn't look like a bruise to me, it looks like a hickey. Your father better not see that or your days of dating that boy are over. I'm not stupid, you know; I was in high school too. Making out is one thing; having sex is another."

"I know, Mom. You've told me a million times and there's nothing going on."

"I hope you would tell me if there was."

Now is the perfect time to tell her, I thought. *Tell her the truth.*

"You need to be honest with me."

"I am, Mom."

She'd kill me if I told her the truth. I wish I had and I wanted to, but I couldn't bring myself to do it. I was having sex and not using birth control. The Catholic Church didn't permit the use of birth control and Mom never used it.

"Children are a gift from God," Mom always said.

I was raised in a strict household with traditional morals and values and I knew right from wrong. The teachings of the Church forbid premarital sex and it never crossed Mom and Dad's mind that I wouldn't be a virgin when I got married. I was taught to live my life the same way Mom and Dad lived theirs, even though I believed they grew up in a world that didn't exist any longer and set an example I couldn't follow. I fought with myself and lied to my parents, hiding the truth I knew would disappoint them. I loved Jack and he loved me and that's what mattered, I told myself.

A. H. Rominger and Sons, circa 1960s

Chapter 16

Jack was off to college in a couple of weeks.

Mom and Dad wouldn't let me date during the week so I said goodnight and went in my room to do my homework. When Donna fell asleep, I locked the door, snuck out the window and drove the Jeep to town to meet Jack. Donna knew I was sneaking out when I woke her up at midnight climbing back through the window.

"Where have you been?" she asked, as she sat up in bed.

"I was cruising around town with Jack. Don't be a tattletale and go running to Mom or I'll tell her about the marijuana."

"She already knows."

"She does not."

"I don't get the big deal about cruising around town in your boyfriend's car. It seems stupid to me."

"When you get a boyfriend you'll understand."

"What's so much fun? I see kids cruising around and they wave to one another and honk their horn. What's so great about that?"

"Just wait until you have a boyfriend."

"What else are you doing? Are you drinking? Are you smoking? Are you making out?"

"You swear you will not say a word to Mom. I'm trusting you Donna. I'll tell Mom you smoked pot at Ursuline."

"I never smoked pot at Ursuline."

"The weekend I came to visit, you snuck out of the room with the other girls, your eyes were bloodshot when you came back, you were laughing like crazy and acting goofy, and I could smell it. So don't sit there like Miss Goody Two-Shoes and tell me you didn't. Anyway, I only had one beer with Jack."

"It's against the law. It's stupid to have beer in the car."

"And smoking pot isn't illegal?"

"You better not be drinking and driving."

"You sound like Mom. Jack and I go to the orchard by low-water bridge with other kids, turn on the stereo and have a few beers. So what?"

"If Mom and Dad find out, you're screwed. You'll be grounded and they won't let you go anywhere. They hate it when we lie to them."

"Just keep your mouth shut."

"My friends and I need a ride home tomorrow night after the game. Can I count on you?"

"So now you're going to blackmail me?" I turned and threw my bed pillow at her. "I'll give your friends a ride home and you keep my secret. Deal?"

"Deal."

I wanted to see Jack as much as I could before he went away. I lied to Mom and Dad and told them I had cheerleading practice at Cathy's house. When I got home and saw them sitting at the kitchen table, I knew I was had.

"Where have you been?" Dad said.

"At Cathy's."

"Don't lie to me. Cathy called here looking for you. Where were you?"

"With Jack."

"Where did you go?"

"What difference does it make?" I started to walk out of the kitchen.

"It makes a lot of difference. You come back here and do not walk away when I am talking to you. No more nights out during the week. Do you hear me? That's final."

"Dad, Jack's leaving for college in less than two weeks."

"Good. How can I trust you if you keep lying to me?"

If Dad knew we were drinking beer and spent most of the time in the back seat of Jack's car having sex, he would shoot me on the spot. Now that he had caught me in a lie, no telling what I'd have to do to get out of the house. I opened the bedroom door and found Donna sitting on the bed.

"You big tattletale. You got me in so much trouble and I have no idea what Dad is going to do, but I haven't heard the last of it. You have a big mouth. I trusted you."

"Don't blame me, you got yourself in this mess. I had no choice. Your dumb girlfriend called here looking for you and Dad stormed down here and insisted I tell him what was going on. What did you want me to do, lie to him? Shit, they aren't stupid. I wasn't about to make up another lie and get in as much trouble as your ass is in."

Mom knocked on the door the next morning. "Get up, it's time for school," she said.

I didn't want to face my parents. I knew I was in deep shit for sneaking out with Jack and lying to them.

"Donna, get in the car with your brothers. Your father is taking you to school this morning," Mom said. "Lorraine, you're not going to school today."

"Why not?"

"We're going to Woodland to see a family counselor. Your father and I are worried about you. You lie to us and we can't trust you and we need some advice. We don't know what to do anymore and we feel like we aren't good parents."

"You're treating me like a criminal and I haven't done anything so terrible that we need a family counselor. I want to hang out with Jack and you don't want me to."

"It's more than that. You were raised to tell the truth." Mom paused. "It's done and the appointment has been made."

I liked the shrink. She wasn't as strict as my parents. She set rules that I said I would follow. Lying was not acceptable.

Jack left for college and I hung out with my girlfriends. Things were fine for a few weeks until I skipped school to go up to the lake to swim and party with the girls and forged a note from my mom saying I was home sick. The school office called Mom to check. It was the lies, my parents said, not that I skipped school. I was grounded for a month.

After a month the shrink told my parents to give me some responsibility, so Dad said I could use the car on Friday night. My girlfriends and I smoked and I was stupid to think four girls could smoke cigarettes in the car and it wouldn't smell the next morning.

"You were smoking in the car last night," Dad said.

"No I wasn't. It wasn't me."

"Who was it?"

"I'm not a tattletale. I'm not telling."

"Fine. There will be no more taking the car out on Friday nights."

"You act like I was doing drugs or something. We tried a cigarette, so what? You smoke. Why are you making such a big deal about it?"

"You're not allowed to smoke," Dad said. "It's illegal, you're underage."

Growing up with strict Catholic parents was not fun. The other girls in my class had their own cars when we were seniors and they smoked and drank and their parents knew what was going on.

I saw the shrink every other week and Mom and Dad didn't want me to see Jack after he left for college. He was a bad influence on me, they said, and they only knew the half of it. They had no idea Jack and I were having sex. Neither did the shrink; I lied to her too.

"I don't think telling Lorraine she can't see Jack any longer is the right thing to do," the shrink said to my parents in our weekly session. "She could leave home and it would be difficult for you to stop her." She turned to me and said, "You know right from wrong and I know kids your age smoke and drink. But you're not old enough to smoke or drink, and having alcohol in the car is unacceptable and dangerous. Trust is earned and I know you want your parents to trust you. In order for that to happen, you have to tell the truth. Let's set rules and boundaries that we can live with. Agreed?"

"OK," I said.

"No more weeknights out. You can see Jack one night on the weekend when he comes home and your curfew is 11:30 p.m. If you go out during the week, one of your parents will take you and pick you up. No more lies and no more alcohol in the car."

I was a senior and having my parents drop me off and pick me up was the ultimate humiliation. Things went along fine until Jack came home for the weekend.

"It's midnight and your curfew is 11:30 p.m.," Dad said, as he got up out of his chair and came toward me. "I can smell beer on your breath."

"Yes, I had a beer. We were at Jack's friend's house, but we didn't have beer in the car. Everyone was drinking at the party, Dad."

"I don't care about everyone. I only care about you, and we had a deal."

"Yes, we had a deal, but we didn't have alcohol in the car. I'm only thirty minutes late."

I was grounded: no going out, no going anywhere, period. Unless Dad took me and picked me up, the only way I could see Jack was if he came to the house. I knew that would go over like a lead balloon; Jack was afraid of Dad.

"Jack, I don't think we should see each other for a while. You're away at college and I'm going to tell my parents we broke up and maybe they'll give me a break and leave me alone."

"Tell them what you want and do what you want. I'm done," Jack said.

I was so upset when Jack hung up the phone. I cried most of the night and Mom wanted to know what was wrong, but I didn't answer her.

Jack called the next morning to apologize. He didn't want to lose me and would do what I wanted, but I lied and told my parents Jack and I decided not to see each other and that was why I was so upset.

"I think it's for the best, honey," Mom said. "He should date girls in college."

Dad was thrilled.

I had no choice but to date other boys, which made my parents happy, but I didn't tell Jack. Mark was tall and handsome and played on the varsity football team, a total babe. I was thrilled when he asked me out after the Homecoming football game and it took me one second to jump in his car. He was a party boy, but loved football and dreamed of playing ball in college. We cruised around Winters and I could imagine what my friends were saying as they passed in their cars, wondering what the hell I was doing with Mark. We turned the corner on Main Street and I spotted Jack's car.

Oh my God, I thought. *He came home to surprise me for Homecoming. What the hell am I going to do? He'll kill me if he sees me in Mark's car.*

"Mark, it's late. I better get home before my parents wonder what happened to me. I told them I'd be home after the game."

Mark dropped me off at my car and kissed me on the cheek. What a dreamboat.

I prayed Jack hadn't seen me in Mark's car as I raced home. When I approached the end of the lane, Jack's car was parked parallel across the road blocking the entrance to our driveway. He was standing beside his car, waiting, and the last thing I was going to do was stop. Jack must have seen me in Mark's car and I knew I was in for a fight.

I thought the driveway was wide enough to get around his car and I swerved to miss it, but caught the back end of his car's rubber bumper. Crash. Jack's car lunged forward and I was so freaked out I didn't stop. I didn't know what to do, so I raced to the house, jumped out of the Jeep and ran in the back door.

"Dad, Dad. I just hit Jack's car. He was blocking the end of the driveway and I tried to swerve around him, but I hit his bumper with the Jeep. He's on his way here and he's pissed off."

I looked out the window as Jack drove up to the back door. Dad said he'd handle it, as he walked outside to clean up my mess, and refused to tell me what was said after Jack pulled away in his car.

"That kid is nuts. I guess this was his last-ditch effort to try and get you back. I'm upset you hit his car, but that boy had no right to block our driveway," Dad said.

Dad paid to fix Jack's car and never brought it up again. That was Dad. He didn't dwell on unpleasant things and had been relieved weeks earlier when I told him Jack and I weren't going out anymore. I tried to forget Jack, but I cared about him. He was handsome and charming and sweet and generous. We had fun together and he was the only boy I'd ever slept with. I fell in love with him long before he laid a hand on me, and my Catholic guilt told me as long as we got married, having sex with him was OK.

Jack had seen me in Mark's car and was pissed off and was even more pissed off that I had sent my Dad out to deal with him after I hit his car. He refused to talk to me the first time I got up the nerve to call to apologize for smashing his car, but not the second time. He apologized too, for trying to block our driveway.

I spent weeks filling out applications to colleges and large envelopes full of information came in the mail. One afternoon I came home from school to find both Mom and Dad sitting at the kitchen table and I knew that look well enough to know I was in trouble. I had no idea how bad it was going to get.

"Come down to our bedroom and close the door," Mom said.

I felt the tension in the air and saw their faces full of disappointment. I had a lump in my throat, my heart was racing and my hands were sweating.

"This came in the mail today," Mom said. "I opened it."

Her hands were shaking and I knew this was going to get ugly. She handed me a large manila envelope with Jack's return address. I looked inside and it was full of the love letters I'd sent him. Jack had been so pissed the night I hit his car that he sent all the letters back before I called to apologize.

Oh shit, I thought. *They know. They know everything.*

"I thought it was from one of the colleges you requested information from so I opened it," Mom said.

"I can't believe you opened my mail. Why would you do that? You knew it was from Jack, it's his return address. You opened it on purpose and you're lying to me, the same thing I get in trouble for."

"Lorraine, how could you have sex with this boy? You're only 17 years old. How many times have I talked to you about having sex before you get married? It's wrong. It's a sin and it's against our faith."

"You read the letters I wrote to Jack? How could you do that? You had no right to open my mail and read the letters I wrote to him!" I screamed, as I yanked the envelope from Mom's hand. "I love him and he loves me. Where does it say it's against our religion to have sex?"

"You thought you were pregnant? You told him that in one of your letters. Why didn't you come to me and talk to me?" Mom said.

"Because I knew you would treat me like you are right now, like I was going straight to hell because I had sex before I was married. I wasn't pregnant, but Jack promised to marry me if I was."

I was hollering and crying at the same time. I was so upset that she and Dad read my letters to Jack and told me they thought the envelope contained one of my college applications.

"Don't be ridiculous," Dad said. "He's 18 and you're 17. You're kids. Do you have any idea what it would be like to have a baby at your age? You are not prepared for that responsibility. Your life would change forever and you would not go to college. Is that what you want?"

"You had just turned twenty when you got married, Mom, and you had a baby at twenty-one," I said.

"Yes, but I didn't sleep with your father until the night we got married. You can't sleep around with boys. It's not right, it's not how you were raised," Mom said, her voice shaking.

"I'm not sleeping around with boys, I slept with Jack. You're living in the Dark Ages. The world has changed since you were in high school," I said, crying.

"It has changed and for the worse. There are certain things you don't do, period, and having sex before you're married is one of them," Mom said.

"You told us you weren't seeing him anymore. You wouldn't even talk to him the night you hit his car," Dad said.

"I was going to tell you. We've been talking and I'm seeing Jack when he comes home next weekend," I cried, as tears ran down my face.

"You're never going to see him again. Not ever. I forbid it," Mom said.

Dad nodded his head back and forth and couldn't even look at me. "It's over."

"You can't stop me from seeing him, you can't. I won't forgive you for opening my mail. You had no right. You just wanted to find out what was in the envelope from Jack."

I was hysterical. I let my parents down and felt so ashamed. But, I was also pissed and knew they had lied to me about opening the envelope from Jack and not knowing it was from him. I stood up from the chair, opened the door and went to my bedroom.

"What's wrong?" Donna said. "Why are you crying? I heard yelling coming from Mom and Dad's room."

"They know I've been sleeping with Jack."

"Holy shit. Are you kidding me? You've been having sex with Jack? Oh my God, you are so dead."

Mom knocked on the door. "Lorraine, come out here. You're coming with me and your father."

"I'm not going anywhere with you."

Dad opened the door. "You're coming with us. Now."

"Where are we going?" I asked, as we got in the car. There was silence as I sat in the back seat. Ten minutes later Dad pulled up in front of the church.

"What are we doing here?"

"We called the priest and Father is waiting to talk to you," Mom said.

"You told Father what I did? How could you do that? It's none of his business."

Silence. There was nothing to say. I had done the worst thing imaginable in my parents' eyes, sleeping with a boy I wasn't married to, and I wasn't a virgin. I got out of the car and stood on the sidewalk. I dreaded talking to the priest.

"Hello, Father," I said, as I walked into his house next to the church. He motioned me to a chair and I sat down, looking at the floor.

What in the hell am I doing here? I asked myself. *Would I leave with a scarlet letter on my chest? Did my parents think confessing my sins to the priest would make it go away? Would I walk out of here forgiven by God?*

"Do you know why you are here?" Father asked.

"Yes. My parents believe I've committed a mortal sin. I had sex with my boyfriend."

"Do you feel you have sinned, Lorraine?" Father asked.

"I know in my parents' eyes I've sinned. I know how hurt and disappointed they are in me and I feel awful about that, Father."

"My child, your parents love you. As does the Lord, no matter what you do. Your parents want what's best for you. Do you understand why they are upset?"

"Because I'm not a virgin anymore. Mom always told me that our faith teaches us we do not have sex until we get married. I feel like that's their rule, not God's. Where does it say that in the Ten Commandments?"

"Abstinence is the teaching of our faith," Father said. And so the conversation went.

"Are you sorry for your sins?" he asked.

"Yes, Father." I had no choice.

"For your penance say the rosary and ask God for his forgiveness."

I wanted to get out of there and go home. I couldn't look at my parents and they didn't look at me.

The next day Mom and Dad took me to see Mrs. Frank, the shrink, and the day after that I packed my bags with my clothes and homework. I moved into a halfway house for troubled kids, kids whose parents didn't know what to do with them and kids whose parents were never home. It was a stop-off between juvenile hall and foster care and I had no idea my shrink ran this home. I was surprised and a little relieved when she came to the door.

"I'll take it from here," Mrs. Frank said to Mom and Dad as we stood on the porch at the front door. "I'll call you in a couple of days and you can come for a session at the end of the week."

I looked at Mom, then at Dad and walked through the door. My stomach was turning and I was upset with my parents for putting me in this place.

"I understand your parents forbid you to see Jack. Why didn't you tell me you were sleeping with him?"

"I didn't want you to know," I said, as I looked at her and paused. "Look, that's the problem. My parents never slept together before they got married and they are devout Catholics. They don't believe in it and they believe I should be a virgin when I get married. I can't imagine marrying someone and not sleeping with them first. And besides, they think all I do is cruise around, drink beer, smoke and cut school. They act like I'm going to hell. I'm not doing anything that most of the girls and boys in my class aren't doing. But I've lied to them so much, they don't believe most of what I say anymore, and they think all of this is their fault. They think they've failed as parents."

"I know kids your age try things. And I do believe your parents have done a good job raising you. Do you think your parents got in trouble when they were young?"

"I'm sure they got in trouble for fighting with their brothers and sisters, but not for drinking and smoking and having sex. I'd bet on that."

"Well, I understand your parents forbid you to see Jack and I told them I think that's a mistake. I'm going to allow you to see him under my conditions. He can come here to visit, but only if you stay in the living room. You are not allowed to leave the house. Do you understand?"

I nodded yes.

"Come on, your room is upstairs."

She led me up a wooden staircase and when I got to the top and looked down, I saw the house was a mess. It was in total disarray. It was no wonder she didn't invite my parents inside. Mom would have taken one look at the place and marched my ass out of there, or so I hoped. Maybe Mom did this on purpose, putting me in this filthy place.

I had a room to myself, but the bathroom was down the hall. There were locks on everything: the bedroom door, the closet, the drawers in the dresser and in the bathroom.

"Why don't you unpack? Dinner will be ready in an hour. Come down to the kitchen at 6 p.m. and you can meet the other kids. I'm sure you're going to like it here."

I closed the door and gazed around the room and felt like I had been dropped off in hell. The room was bare and cold: a bed, a dresser, a nightstand and a lamp. No pictures on the walls, no rugs on the floor, and the sheets and blankets were old and worn. I put my things in the closet and dresser and locked them with the key. I sat down on the bed as tears rolled down my face.

God, I asked myself, *is having sex with my boyfriend a mortal sin?* My girlfriends were having sex and I wondered if their parents knew. They must know. My girlfriends went away for the weekend with their boyfriends, but none of my girlfriends were Catholics.

I had my homework assignments for two months. Mom took care of that with my teachers and I wasn't sure what she told them—maybe that I was going off on a study course abroad. She wouldn't tell me and it was better I didn't know. It would have pissed me off. At 6 p.m., I opened the door and walked downstairs to the kitchen. The kids were outside playing when I arrived earlier and the house had been quiet, but now there was commotion, yelling, laughing and orders being given by an aide who worked in the house.

"All right, let's sit down. Stop that and sit in your regular seat. Put that away and do as you're told. Everyone, please pay attention. We have a new girl who arrived today and I want you to say hello to Lorraine."

It was total pandemonium. There were fifteen kids in the house and a six-month-old baby in the high chair. I was, without a doubt, the oldest. There was a cook, an aide and the shrink to take care of these kids. I knew what I was in for, babysitting and cleaning house.

I guessed a few of the kids were toddlers, a few of them in grammar school and a few of them in junior high. "So what did you do to end up in this place?" the young girl sitting next to me whispered.

"I had a terrible fight with my parents. They think I'm going to hell."

"Well, at least you have parents. Most of the time I came home to an empty house and never knew where my parents were. They drank and did drugs all day. To tell you the truth, I don't care. At least here I'm not alone and there's food on the table."

Boy, did that make me feel like shit. I had parents who were around all the time and wanted to know my every move. "Do you like it here?"

"Mrs. Frank is finding me a foster family to live with so I don't plan to be here much longer."

"I hope she finds you a wonderful family." I thought about my family eating dinner at home together around the kitchen table. I wondered what Mom and Dad would say to Donna, Joe and Dan about me not being home.

The kids in the home were from the area and got on the bus in the morning to go to school. I didn't leave to go to school and was stuck in the house all day. I tried to do my homework, but there was a baby and several toddlers in the house, and one of them was always crying.

I had helped out at home and taken care of my sister and brothers, and I couldn't sit with kids crying and a baby that needed changing. There were dishes in the sink and piles of dirty clothes in the laundry room. Mrs. Frank said there were more kids in the house than usual and they were good kids, but had been neglected by their parents and had no one to turn to for love and support. I felt sorry for them and realized my troubles weren't as bad as I thought. My parents were strict, but I knew they loved me. I spent several hours a day cleaning, doing laundry and taking care of the kids.

Jack came to visit and we argued. Things were not the same between us. It's hard to take back hurtful things, no matter how many times you apologize; the hole is always there. He was angry at me for going out with Mark and I felt bad for hurting him, but I was sick of the fights and my feelings for him weren't the same. His feelings for me had changed too.

When my parents told me I couldn't see Jack, all I wanted to do was figure out ways to see him. I distinctly remember Mrs. Frank's words to my parents, "If you tell her to do one thing, she will almost always do another."

Now that I was allowed to see him, I didn't want to.

After the kids went to bed, Mrs. Frank and I talked. "Shall I call your parents and ask them to come over this week for a visit? I thought you might want to see them."

"I'd like to wait. They're probably glad they don't have to deal with me."

"Your parents love you and want you to be happy. They only want what's best for you. Sometimes a little distance can help you see the situation more clearly."

"I know."

Mom brought my sewing machine and patterns and material to me in the halfway house so I had something to do besides homework. I had taken sewing classes in 4-H and spent hours in high school making my own dresses. I had won a purple ribbon for "Best in Show" at the Yolo County Fair in Woodland for a tailored, lined wool coat that took me weeks to make. I remember attending monthly 4-H meetings in my white blouse and skirt, my green wraparound belt and green 4-H hat with a stripe for each year of service sewn on my hat with my achievement medals pinned on the stripes. I kept the hat.

I was lucky to have a Mom and Dad who would do anything for me. I did a crappy job living up to their expectations, but Dad expected me to be perfect and I wasn't. Still, they didn't give up on me and I knew they sacrificed so my sister and brothers and I could have the things we wanted. Here I was in a house full of unwanted kids who made me feel lucky.

Reality hit me square in the face the next morning when a 16-year-old girl named Erin who was five months pregnant came to live in the house. Her parents had kicked her out because they wanted her to have an abortion. Mrs. Frank agreed to help her and I thanked God it wasn't me.

I spent over a month in the halfway house and Mom and Dad came to visit once a week.

"I'm sorry I'm a disappointment and I'm sorry I lied to you. I hope you'll forgive me."

"You are not a disappointment, but the things you did were disappointing. We love you and want you to finish high school and get a college education," Mom said.

"Mrs. Frank thinks you should come home," Dad said. "It will be good to have you where you belong."

I put my arms around Dad and hung on for dear life, and then I turned to Mom and hugged her. Living in the halfway house had been good for me and I realized my parents were raising me the best way they knew how, and most of the time they were right. I told the kids I was going home and felt guilty for leaving. Mrs. Frank said Erin decided to keep the baby. Mom and Dad were right; having a baby at a young age changes your life. There's no going back. Kids are forever.

"So, what was it like in the nut house?" Donna said, when I got home. "Did they lock you in your room?"

"I wasn't in a nut house. I was in a halfway home with fifteen kids whose parents didn't want them and I spent most of my time cleaning, changing diapers and babysitting."

"Well, you're good at that. Did you learn your lesson?"

"What lesson is that, Miss Smarty Pants?"

"That you better not lie to Mom and Dad and have sex with your boyfriend."

"I don't have a boyfriend. And yes, I learned my lesson."

"I learned my lesson too. Better tow the line around here. Don't forget, I went away to boarding school for a year."

"You were hell on wheels in eighth grade and you wanted to go to boarding school." I paused. "You know, the home wasn't as bad as it could have been." We looked at each other and smiled. "I missed you and I'm glad to be home."

"I missed you too...but not as much as I loved having the room to myself."

I picked up my pillow and blasted her with it.

"Some things never change," Donna said, laughing.

Dad holding his tomatoes

Chapter 17

My high school days were coming to an end and I'd be off to college in a few months.

One of my girlfriends threw a slumber party for the senior girls and we were sitting on Stacey's front porch listening to music when a carload of senior boys pulled in the driveway and opened their trunk with an ice chest full of beer. Who should drive by as I took a beer out of the ice chest, but my uncle who drove straight to his house and called my Dad. Within fifteen minutes, Dad was knocking on Stacey's front door.

"Dad, what are you doing here?"

"You're coming home with me. Let's go. Get in the car."

"Dad, you are being unreasonable."

"How many times have I told you? You are not allowed to drink until you are twenty-one, period. Your Mom and I never drank in high school. There were no beer bottles sitting on the tables at our parties, just bottles of Coke and potato chips."

"Dad, the world was a different place twenty years ago when you and Mom were in high school."

"It's the law. It was the law back then and it's the law now. There's nothing more to say."

I felt like I had a rope around my neck.

Girls asked boys to the Sadie Hawkins dance and I didn't have a boyfriend, so I went with Mary. We were in the bathroom with a bunch of girls laughing and joking about the new girls' locker room, how sterile it was with its white walls and gray metal lockers and how much we missed the character of the old gymnasium where our dads had played ball. We'd been drinking and I was showing off, wearing my new cowgirl boots. We were dancing and kicking our feet in the air and the next thing I knew, my footprint was in the plaster wall under the huge mirror in the alcove where the girls fixed their hair and makeup. The plaster crumbled and fell to the floor.

"What happened?" Mary said. "What did you do?"

"I was just horsin' around. Hell, in the old gymnasium the walls were made of steel. That wall is made of paper and I can't believe my foot went right through it. Oh my God, I am in such deep shit."

I knew there'd be hell to pay come Monday when I went to school. The hole in the wall would take some explaining.

"Hey girls, how about a beer?" a couple of boys in our class asked as we ran out the back door of the gym and approached their car next to the Jeep. "Come on, let's head out to the orchard."

The boys handed Mary a six-pack. "Mary, what are you doing? Don't put that beer in the Jeep."

"I'll hide it under the seat."

We neglected to see the cop car sitting across the street and less than a mile out of town, the red light went on behind me. "Shit, what did I do wrong?"

"Those damn cops must have been across the street from the high school parking lot," Mary said.

"Fuck, where's that beer? What are you doing?" as Mary started throwing the beer cans out the window. "The cop can see the cans flying through the air."

"Better out there than in here," Mary said, as I came to a stop.

I looked in my rear-view mirror and saw the Chief picking up the beer cans on the side of the road. "Did you girls lose something?" the Chief of Police asked, as he stood next to the Jeep with beer cans in his hands, one leaking from being thrown on the ground. I didn't know if his being my godfather would help me or not.

I hung my head on the steering wheel. *Holy shit*, I thought.

"How many beers have you girls had tonight?" the Chief asked.

I didn't say a word as he shined the flashlight in my face. "Lorraine, I want you to turn this Jeep around and go home. I'll give your Dad a call in the morning."

"Please don't call my Dad, Chief."

"Go home. Be glad it was me that stopped you."

I dropped Mary off at her house and couldn't blame her for not wanting to spend the night. The morning would not be pleasant once my godfather called Dad.

I walked in the kitchen the next morning. I hadn't slept. "Dad, you're going to get a call from the Chief."

"I already did. Do you want to tell me what happened last night?"

"I think you already know."

"What were you thinking throwing the beer out the window? What were you doing with beer in the Jeep in the first place? Who bought it for you?"

"The boys had it and I knew the minute I put it in the Jeep, it was a mistake."

"Then why did you do it? When are you going to learn? No car and no nights out. You're grounded."

"Dad, come on. Can't you give me a break?"

"Give you a break? Be glad your godfather pulled you over or you'd be in jail for possession and I'd be bailing you out."

Yeah, he didn't know the half of it yet.

"You've got to tell Mom and Dad what happened in the gym bathroom," Donna said. "Kids in school know about it and you better not wait until Monday morning. Dad is going to kill you, but you might save your ass a pinch if you tell him now."

"I know, I'll tell him. I'm not going to get out of this house until graduation."

All day I thought about how to tell them and there was no way to sugarcoat how I kicked a hole in the gym wall. After dinner I went in the den where my parents were watching television and felt like I was confessing to the priest.

"Mom, Dad. I have something I need to tell you and you're not going to be happy." They looked at me without saying a word. "I did a little damage in the girls' locker room last night."

"You did what?" Dad asked.

"A bunch of us girls were screwing around in the locker room and I kicked the wall with my new boot and my foot went right through the plaster. I didn't mean to do it, Dad, it just happened."

"How many beers did you have?"

I didn't answer. I didn't have to.

"Did you tell the chaperone at the dance what happened?" Dad asked.

"No, I didn't want anyone to know."

"You didn't want anyone to know. Is that all you have to say for yourself?"

Dad just stared at me and Mom didn't say a word. I think at this point nothing would have surprised them. "I'll take you to school Monday morning and you'll go to the principal's office and tell him what happened."

"Will you go with me?"

"No. You got yourself into this mess and you're going to get yourself out of it. You'll pay to fix the hole because I'm not paying for it."

Just as I had guessed, I was grounded for the rest of the year.

When I got to the principal's office Monday morning and asked to see him, it was clear from the look on his face he knew.

"The janitor called me over the weekend after he cleaned up the mess and patched the hole. You need to tell me what happened," the principal said.

There was no explaining the hole in the wall.

"I'm suspending you from school for three days. The hole is being repaired this morning and you will reimburse the school for damages. In addition, you will not be playing in the girls' basketball tournament this weekend."

"That's not fair. I've been practicing all year for this tournament and I'm the captain of the team."

"You should have thought about that. Your behavior is unacceptable."

Keep your mouth shut, I said to myself. *Just shut up.*

I went straight home and told Dad.

"I knew he was going to suspend me and make me pay to fix the wall. But he has no right to kick me off the team. It's not fair, Dad."

"This is a good lesson. Maybe you'll think twice next time before you do something so stupid. One thing is for sure, they won't win the tournament without you."

That night lying in bed I was so pissed off I couldn't sleep. I heard Mom and Dad in the next room. I couldn't tell what they were saying, but Dad was on my side and that surprised me. He was furious I had beer in the Jeep, but he loved sports, it was one thing I did well and he was proud of that. Plus, Dad didn't have much respect for the principal. The next day Mom and Dad made an appointment with the principal and I have no idea what kind of deal Dad made, or if Mom had influence over him because she was on the school board. Didn't matter. I played in the basketball tournament and we won the championship. Dad was happy with me, that day anyway.

Seventy seniors graduated in my class. I didn't get straight *A*'s like Donna and Joe did when they graduated from high school. They were both valedictorians of their classes; they got the brains in the family. I was nervous about leaving and going to college; I didn't know any place other than the farm and Winters. High school had been a blast, and even though I had my share of ups and downs, I had one happy and rowdy childhood.

The world awaiting me was different than our world on the farm, and much different than the world my parents grew up in; their world was vanishing. Society challenged the family unit and families were separating and falling apart. People weren't dedicated to each other, Mom said, like they used to be. Mom had always encouraged me to go away to college, dream big and travel the world. We spent hours together looking through the encyclopedias at far-off places and capitals of other countries, and she encouraged all of us kids from a young age to do things she had never done. I knew the only way I would stay in Winters was if I became a farmer or married one. As much as I loved the farm, I wanted to experience more in life than Winters had to offer.

As a young girl, my Mom had dreamed of being a singer and an actress. She had a great voice and sang in the church choir and was the lead in school plays. But Mom was also an old-fashioned girl who got married three weeks after her 20th birthday and devoted her life to Dad and us kids. Dad only wanted to live on the farm where he'd spent his whole life.

"What could be better than working the land and being a farmer? Why would you want to live in a city when you can live here?" Dad asked.

Dad thought I'd be a great farmer. But I wasn't going to be a farmer and come back to Winters after college. I wanted to see the world, though I also wanted to get married and have kids, just like Mom and Dad.

All of us kids worked side by side on the farm that summer from sunup to sundown just as we'd done since grammar school. Joe and Dan and Donna and I worked in the fields. We could drive just about any piece of equipment on the farm, and so could Rick and Charlie and Ruth and Bruce. If we didn't know how to operate it, our dads taught us. Not more than a few days after school was out, we started harvesting the barley and wheat. I was sitting in the grain truck waiting for a load as Joe moved the John Deere harvester into a new wheat field and cut a header around the perimeter. The canal we skied in ran along one side of the field. Joe made a couple of rounds and motioned Donna to move the bank out wagon closer to the harvester so he could dump the load. She didn't see him and suddenly he threw open the cab door and scrambled down the steps of the harvester.

"What the hell are you doing over there? Move closer so I can dump the load before I turn around."

There was a dip at the edge of the field before the dirt rose several inches to a crest and then dropped straight into the canal. The wheels of the harvester began to roll forward following the contour of the land, gaining momentum as it rolled to the top of the crest and began to teeter from the weight of the header.

"Joe, the harvester!" Donna screamed, pointing. "Joe!"

We stood in disbelief as the harvester teetered forward, then rolled back a few inches from the crest at the canal's edge. *Oh thank God,* I thought, *it won't fall in the canal.* But the weight of the header proved too great.

"Joe, the harvester!" Donna screamed again.

The harvester took a nosedive straight into the canal, the header sliding down the muddy bank, pulling the harvester with it, slamming on the bottom, bending the header like a pop-top on a beer can. With a crashing thud, the header rested in the canal bottom, the back wheels of the harvester spinning three feet in the air as water and mud flew in every direction.

"Fuck!" Joe yelled.

"Dad is going to kill us!" Donna yelled.

"If you'd been watching me none of this would've happened."

"Don't blame this shit on me."

Dad came barreling down the canal bank a few hundred yards in front of us. Dust was flying and we could barely see the pickup through the clouds.

"Oh shit," Donna said. "What are we going to tell him?"

"Tell him what? He's going to kill me!" Joe screamed.

It was all I could do to keep a straight face as Joe and Donna stood there with Dad's harvester mangled, hunched over itself in the bottom of the canal, still running. The pickup came to a screeching halt and Dad jumped out, grabbed the hat off his head and threw it on the ground.

"Goddammit. Jesus Christ. What the hell did you do?" Dad said.

We were flabbergasted. It was the first time in our life we had heard our Dad swear. That was as hard to believe as the harvester lying in the bottom of the canal.

"What were you thinking? Don't you have a brain in your head? Do you know how much that harvester costs? How in the hell do you think you're going to get it out of the bottom of that damn canal? What happened?"

"I got off the harvester to tell Donna where to park and I must have left it in neutral."

"You mean to tell me you didn't set the brake?"

"The field's flat, Dad."

"How can the damn field be flat if the harvester's in the bottom of the canal? Didn't I teach you anything?" Dad rubbed his head, staring at the wheels spinning in the air. "Get in the truck. We'll have to go to the shop and get the D-6 to pull it out."

It wasn't until the next morning the harvester was on the canal bank and within an hour on the lowbed truck headed for the John Deere dealer. Joe learned an expensive lesson that day. One thing I will say about Dad, when it was over and done, it was over. He didn't dwell on things. Dad was never one to rub our faces in it. He'd get mad, tell us what we should have done, what was going to happen as a consequence and move on.

"Making people feel humiliated over and over when they make a mistake destroys their self-confidence," Dad said. "You need to learn from your mistakes and not dwell on them. A smart man doesn't make the same mistake twice."

When grain harvest ended, tomato harvest started and I was the only girl driving the tractor-trailer that hauled tomatoes out of the field. The trailers hooked up to semi-trucks that hauled the tomatoes to the cannery. Men didn't like working with a girl and they liked it even less that I was the owner's daughter. Dad said they didn't like me because I was a better driver, but I knew they didn't like me because I was Dad's eyes in the field when he wasn't around. Dad wanted to know which workers didn't pull their weight and I told him.

Before tomato harvest started, Dad took me out in the field and taught me to drive the tractor-trailer. "You have to use common sense. The end of the field is uneven and muddy where we closed the irrigation ditch and it's easy to jackknife the trailer full of tomatoes if you don't pay attention. The trailer will sink in the soft dirt when it's heavy and full of fruit."

I never spilled one tomato, but I watched men get fired for dumping tons of tomatoes on the ground. Driving the tractor-trailer was a lot easier than standing on the tomato harvester all day sorting tomatoes. A large circular blade cut the tomato vine off just under the ground and the vine was then carried onto a belt that vibrated and shook the tomatoes off the vine, dropping them onto another conveyor belt where six men stood to sort out green tomatoes, dirt clods and whatever other things were mixed in with the red tomatoes that didn't belong. The conveyor belt moved the good, red tomatoes onto another belt that dumped the tomatoes into the gigantic bin on the trailer pulled by the tractor. Standing on the harvester all day in the heat and the dust and the noise was not an easy job. The men wore gloves so the juice from the tomatoes didn't eat the skin off their fingers and hands, and they wore clothes to cover every inch of their body to keep them cool, as well as a mouth mask to keep them from eating dirt and dust. All the tomatoes my Dad grew, whether they were organic or conventional, were planted and harvested with machines and oblong in shape with hard skins so they weren't crushed going through the harvester or piled on top of one another in the trailer. One of my Dad's friends, Bob Button, a farmer who lived just down the road from us, invented one of the first mechanical tomato harvesters in the early 1960s that my Dad used to harvest his tomatoes.

After tomato harvest was over, I drove the alfalfa rake. It was not my favorite job, but I never told Dad. The alfalfa had been cut with the swather and left in three-foot windrows to dry in the field. Depending on the weather, the hay took three to four days to dry. It was my job to rake three windrows of hay into one larger windrow using the 30-foot wheel rake attached to the John Deere tractor. The hay had to be damp when it was raked or the leaves would fall off, so I worked in the middle of the night when it was cool. Dad checked the moisture before bed and I was up at two in the morning and worked until after the sun came up. I dreaded driving in the field in the pitch black to start the old tractor. Animals rustled in the hay rows and I heard coyotes howl. After an hour or two, I had to force myself to stay awake and it was hard to see in the pitch black.

"Do the best you can," Dad said.

"But Dad, the light on the tractor isn't bright enough. Sometimes I can't tell where I am and I'm afraid I'll run into the ditch at the end of the field."

If I turned the tractor too sharp at the end of the field, the rake whipped the windrows apart and made it impossible for Dad to bale the hay.

"What were you doing last night?" Dad asked. "I spent more time on the ground with the pitchfork fixing the rows at the end of the field than I did sitting on the tractor pulling the baler."

When Dad was a little boy they didn't have motorized equipment and used mules to pull the ground powered blade on wheels, controlled with a foot lever to cut the hay and an attached seat for the operator to sit on. The workers used pitchforks to pile the hay in shocks, little mounds scattered across the field, and after the hay cured in the shocks a few days later, the workers used a pitchfork to load the shocks on a horse-drawn wagon. The farmhands made 65 cents an hour and Dad and his brother and sister made 22 cents an hour, because Grandpa said it took the three of them to do the work of one farmhand.

Dad and Aunt Claire and Uncle Richard made extra money by killing gophers that made a mess in the alfalfa field. After making a levee around the gopher hole, they filled the hole with water and when the gopher came out of the hole, Dad hit it with a shovel and Grandpa gave him a nickel for each gopher. I never would have made it as a farmer back in those days if I'd had to use a pitchfork to load the hay on the wagon and kill gophers with a shovel.

Dad also grew test plots of Crenshaw melons for the University of California at Davis. The university experimented with fertilizers, pesticides and irrigation techniques and when the melons ripened and were ready to harvest, the university had finished the tests and didn't want the fruit.

"There's ten acres of ripe melons in the field and they're going to rot," Dad said. "If you take care of them, you can sell them and keep the money. It's up to you."

"It's a deal, Dad. I'll do it. I'll pick the melons and sell them."

I had no idea how much work I got myself into. The vines had been trampled and the melons in the field were exposed to the scorching sun. I planned to sell them at the farmer's market, so to minimize the sun spots, I had to spray each melon with whitewash. I had to pick, clean, size, weigh, pack and haul them to market. I babied those melons and agonized over them, as each one was worth several cents a pound. Hundreds of them covered the floor in the living room as I weighed each one on Mom's bathroom scale. By the time I finished loading and packing the melons in the truck, I was sick of them.

I drove an hour to Sacramento, carefully. No one buys bruised or spotted melons at the farmer's market because people expect the fruit to look perfect or they think they aren't getting their money's worth. Since we didn't have fruit boxes, I had to wrap each melon in newspaper and pack them one by one in rows in Dad's pickup—and the truck was filled to the side rails with hundreds of melons. The market opened at 6 a.m. and by 2 p.m., I'd sold my last melon and raced home to count my money.

"How much money did you make?" Dad asked.

"Almost $800. I have enough money to buy a new car."

The next day, Dad and I went to the Ford dealer and ordered a sea-foam green, brand-new Mustang. Mr. Graf, who owned the dealership, was related to Mom's side of the family and said the car would arrive at the beginning of September, just in time before I left for college. I couldn't wait.

Miss Sugar Queen Pageant, 1971

Chapter 18

Momo and Popo had retired, bought an Airstream trailer and moved to Mesa.

Later that summer, we piled in Dad's Ford and drove from California to Arizona in one day. Dad was never one to dillydally.

We left in the middle of the night, with us kids in our pajamas and Mom in the front seat being a good sport, not complaining. Dad hated to stop once we got on the road and if we had to pee, he made a contest out of seeing who could hold it the longest. Thank God Mom's bladder didn't work so well after having four kids. Dad only stopped when Mom said she was going to pee her pants. When we arrived, Popo and Momo were sitting on the porch of the trailer with their little black poodle on Popo's lap.

"You kids have changed and grown up so much, I can hardly believe my eyes," Momo said.

"We miss you since you moved to Arizona and we miss our hunting and fishing trips," Joe said, as he ran to them and jumped on Popo.

Popo retold the stories about the trips with my brothers when they were little, the rocks catching fire in the sleeping bag and the buck walking through camp with Dad's gun lying on the table, and we laughed again at the same old stories. Popo couldn't stop talking about the past, but we didn't care, he could talk about whatever he wanted. Popo had colon cancer and didn't have long to live and Mom said we shouldn't mention the cancer because Popo didn't want to talk about it. When it was time to go home, none of us wanted to leave; we were afraid we wouldn't see Popo again. He stood at the end of the driveway waving goodbye in his black pants and flannel shirt, the clothes hanging on his thin body.

I turned 18 in Arizona and Mom and Dad surprised us when we left Momo and Popo's.

"We're going home through Las Vegas," Dad announced. "We bought tickets to see Sonny and Cher to celebrate your 18th birthday."

Donna and I never missed Sonny and Cher's weekly television show; we thought we were their biggest fans. The dinner ballroom at Caesar's was packed. Cher was breathtaking, with her long, black straight hair, big hoop earrings, and midriff outfit baring her stomach. I couldn't figure out what she saw in Sonny; he couldn't carry a tune in a bucket.

"She made him a star," Dad said. "He'd be nothing without her, but she'd be something without him."

We ended the trip like we started, leaving at the crack of dawn with Dad in a hurry to get home and us kids wondering why we couldn't sleep in when we were on vacation. One thing we could count on, after a few days on the road, Dad was itching to get home.

College started the next week and I lived off campus in a private housing complex at Sacramento State that was similar to an apartment, but it was better than an apartment. There wasn't a kitchen and I didn't have to cook, and I ate in a fancy cafeteria. Eight girls shared four bedrooms, a huge bathroom and a living room; it was expensive and the best place to live. Mom and Dad sacrificed so I could live at Westbridge where there were after-school activities, a swimming pool and a gym. I took a part-time job after school to earn extra spending money, against Mom and Dad's wishes.

"You'll have enough to do with your studies and we don't want you to worry about how you're going to pay for things," Mom said. "We can afford to pay for your education, and your Dad and I want you to devote your time to studying and getting good grades. Nothing is more important."

"Except making the basketball team," Dad added.

I majored in Physical Education. My dream was to be a professional woman athlete and play basketball. After all, I came from a family of jocks, and one thing I did well, and loved to do, was play sports. I grew up a tomboy, always competing with the boys on the ranch and working in the fields. Dad said I was fast and tough, could hold my own and had great hand-eye coordination.

Dad, Joe and Dan helped me move "my crap," as Dad called it, to Sacramento. We looked like the Beverly Hillbillies pulling into the parking lot in a two-ton flatbed truck, the load tied down with ropes.

"You better not plan on moving," Dad said. "I've never seen so much crap for one student in my life. I had one suitcase when I went to Davis."

"You're a guy, Dad. Girls need more stuff," I said, as Dad, Joe and Dan spent three hours unloading the truck carrying boxes, furniture, suitcases and plants into my room.

I was nervous about leaving home; I'd never left the farm for any length of time without my family. The first grandchild to go to college, I knew my whole family was watching me. I'd spent my life on the farm with my sister, brothers, parents, aunts, uncles, cousins and grandparents.

A few days after school started, Dad called. "You need to come home this weekend."

"It's my car. Did it come in? Have you seen it?" I asked, excited in a loud voice.

"Yep, it's here. I'll be over Friday to bring you home."

No more clunkers, no more farm hand-me-downs. My very own, brand-new Ford Mustang. Dad and I walked into the Ford dealer Saturday morning as I turned my head, scouring the showroom with my eyes.

"Well, where is it? I don't see it."

"It's right there. It's that one," Dad said, as he pointed to something green.

"That's not the car I ordered. It doesn't look anything like last year's model. That's not the car I saw in the book."

"Well," said Mr. Graf, "it's a new decade and Ford decided to change the body style."

"It's totally different than the '69 Mustang." I looked at Dad with disappointment, scrunched up my nose and let out a sigh.

It looks like a space mobile, it's ugly. *That can't be my car*, I thought, as my heart sank. I worked for years to earn the money and I wanted the car I ordered.

"Don, if she doesn't want the car, I'm sure I can sell it," Mr. Graf said.

"You'll learn to love it," Dad whispered. "You know the thing about a car? It's not what it looks like that counts. It's that it gets you from point *A* to point *B* with no problems."

"No," I said to Mr. Graf. "It's great. I'll take it." I wrote a check for $3,300 and drove off in a spanking brand-new car. I'll learn to love it, I told myself.

My roommate in college was one of my best friends from high school. We were born on the same day, dated boys from our rival high school, were song leaders together and had the same friends. The first day of school as we ate lunch in the cafeteria, one of the best-looking guys I'd ever seen was standing at the milk machine with four glasses of milk on his tray.

"Virginia. Look at the guy at the milk machine in the maroon and white sweater."

"You think his pants could be any tighter?"

"He must work out, look at his arms. I'm going to marry him one day."

"Oh shit, you're not going to marry him. You don't even know him. He could be an ax murderer for God's sake," she said, as she stood up and started to clear her tray from the table.

"I'm going to get to know him and he's going to get to know me. You wait and see," I said, as I followed her out the door.

Getting to know him wasn't easy. He was shy and I didn't see him around the complex, except by the pool. It took several times running into him to get up the nerve to introduce myself.

"Is something wrong?" I asked, as I looked up and saw him standing over me as I lay on the lounge chair. "Is this your book? I thought someone left it here." I was lying. I'd seen him lay the book down on the chair before he got in the pool. "Are you a business major?" I asked, as I examined the cover and handed it to him.

"Trying to be. Not sure I picked the right major," he said.

"Yeah, me either. I'm Lorraine."

"I'm Craig."

The next night he took me to get an ice-cream and I knew he was the one. Craig was tall, dark and handsome, kind and polite. His family lived in the San Joaquin Valley and owned a lumber company. Craig had his pilot's license and flew his Dad's plane and drove a cool sports car. He was a big game hunter and traveled the world with his Dad and his uncle collecting animal trophies. The thought of that made me sick and I couldn't understand why anyone would want to travel the world and kill animals, but I let that slip. It reminded me of Dad, although we ate the animals Dad killed. Dad never made stuffed trophies of the animals he shot.

My first year of college was everything I dreamed it would be. I was dating a total babe, made the women's basketball and field hockey teams as a starter, and got all A's and B's. I took Craig home to meet my parents and they liked him, especially Dad. They talked about guns and hunting, and he got along great with my brothers.

I looked forward to spending the summer on the ranch. I missed my sister and brothers and wanted to sleep in my bed in my room and work for Dad on the farm. Donna and I drove grain trucks, racing through the day to see who could haul the most loads of barley to the bins. Not much had changed except we were growing up and Joe got stuck driving the bank out wagon. It was a relief to know that every summer when school got out I had a job on the farm and didn't have to spend time applying for work.

Dad worked in the fields all day and we couldn't keep up with him, and Mom got up at the crack of dawn, cooked our breakfast and made our lunch so we could work all day in the fields. Dad was a slave driver, but he did take a lunch break for 15 minutes. Rick and Charlie drove harvesters that summer and Ruth drove the truck. We'd sit underneath the harvester in the shade and I swear Dad inhaled his food; he was the fastest eater I'd ever seen. He was the first one finished every day and we had to beg him to give us a few more minutes to eat. Dad and Uncle Richard grew a few thousand acres of barley and wheat and we spent six weeks harvesting from the day we got out of school. Dad ran the field operations and Uncle Richard ran the office and kept all the books. Dan was only nine that summer and he and Bruce were too young to work in harvest. As time passed and my cousins grew up, it wasn't long before my aunts' kids, Matt, Tommy, Diana and Corinne, were working in the fields too.

Growing up on the farm, we never slept in. Dad said it was better to get going early when it's cool. Even today, I can't sleep in. If we weren't out of bed by 6 a.m., there was a loud knock on our wooden bedroom door. Nothing said, just the knock that continued until one of us groaned, "OK, Dad."

If we didn't respond to the knock, Dad opened the door and grabbed the ends of our feet as if to pull us out of bed. "No rest for the wicked," he said.

My sophomore year, I became a resident assistant at Westbridge and was on call 24 hours a day, in charge of the students who lived in my building. Being a resident assistant, I was given a student discount and a room to myself. Craig moved to an apartment off campus and we stopped seeing each other. I was upset, but he wanted to date other girls and his roommate was a party boy and they were stoned every time I went to their apartment.

Being a resident assistant was more work and responsibility than I thought it would be, and loads of fun. There were eight small buildings within the large complex and a resident assistant lived in each building. An older couple managed the complex and their influence helped me become a better person. The resident assistants spent hours together in meetings, sharing our likes, our dislikes, our problems and our successes. I grew up that year and benefited from the close group of people I trusted and respected, who trusted and respected me. As the youngest resident assistant, the advice from older and more experienced coworkers was priceless.

My days were spent studying, babysitting the students in my building and playing sports. I spent too much time rescuing drunk freshman, which made me think of my high school days and what a drag my drinking must have been for my parents.

Our field hockey team went undefeated. Most of the credit went to our coach, a woman I came to love and admire. Of all my teachers in college she was the kindest, fairest and most inspirational, all the things I wanted to be. I learned a great deal from Miss Hughes. I became more than teammates with several girls on the team, friendships I kept long after college.

I looked forward to game day and during warmup my eyes focused on the sideline until I spotted Dad and Mom. Dad never missed a home game and that meant a great deal to me, almost as much as winning. I wanted Dad and Mom to be proud of me. I had become more of the person they wanted me to be: mindful, respectful and a practicing Catholic, living my life by my Catholic upbringing.

"Great game, Lorr. You outran the girl down the field every time you got the ball," Dad said. "I'm proud of you. You played a great game. I hope you're behaving yourself," he added, as he put his arm around me and patted me on the back. "Going to church every Sunday, I hope."

"Yes Dad, every Sunday."

At the end of my sophomore year, I moved out of Westbridge and rented an apartment for the fall with a girlfriend. It was time to get my own place, cook for myself and be on my own. Craig came back into my life, said he missed me, got tired of partying and dating other girls, and by summer we were spending weekends together. He had two younger sisters and a younger brother, but Craig was his mother's favorite and she made no bones about it.

During a weekend at their house, I overheard a conversation his Mom was having with her friend on the phone. "She's not what I had in mind for my son. Her father is a dirt farmer. I want better than that for Craig."

I wanted Craig all the more. I'll show her, I promised myself. She'll regret the day she said that about my Dad. Craig and I grew closer that summer and had serious discussions about marriage.

Every summer our family went to the Yolo County Fair, the biggest event in the county. The fair was more than food booths and amusement rides, from 4-H exhibits, farm animal competitions, tractor pulls and a rodeo to drag races, cookoffs, food competitions and a beauty pageant—an authentic county fair. Packed with rides and prize booths, if you could throw a dime and land it on a thin, slippery plate, you had your choice of any oversized stuffed animal you wanted. Dad was great at pitching dimes and Donna and I grew up with a room full of the stuffed animals he won at the county fair.

"Lorraine, one of my friends in the Elks Club called today. They want you to represent them in the Sugar Queen contest and compete for Miss Yolo County at the county fair," Dad said.

"It's an honor to be asked," Mom said. "You should be proud of yourself."

All contestants in the pageant were sponsored by local organizations. The unofficial title was Miss Sugar Queen, and my brothers nicknamed the pageant Miss Sugar Beet and teased me relentlessly. I paid no attention to them. As a kid, I had sat in front of the television with my legs crossed, my eyes glued to the set watching the Miss USA Pageant and dreaming of being a contestant one day. The winner of the Sugar Queen contest represented Yolo County in the Maid of California pageant the opening night of the State Fair in Sacramento and at the Miss California Pageant in Los Angeles. I prepared all summer, went on a diet and ran several miles a day after driving the grain truck during the harvest. Joe and Dan made fun of me.

"There goes Lorraine walking down the hall, practicing her turns to be Miss Sugar Beet. Why do you want to be in that stupid beauty pageant anyway?" Joe asked.

I ignored him. He was a boy; what did he know about what girls wanted to do?

As a contestant, I was required to attend meetings, sign a contract and abide by the rules, and I took this seriously. I made my own evening gown for the competition: a sleeveless ivory crepe gown, with a V-neck, and flowing skirt. It fit like a glove. I was 5'10" and the tallest girl in the pageant and had the hardest time deciding what to do with my long dark hair. Should I wear it up or down? I ended up wearing it down.

I wanted to win. Nothing was more important to me than representing the county where I was born and raised. Thirty girls entered the pageant from various towns in the county. The night of the pageant I was a nervous wreck, and when my name was announced as the contestant who sold the most tickets, I went on stage to receive the award and tripped over the sound cord and nearly fell on my face. I'd never been so embarrassed in my life, well maybe except the day I cut my legs shaving with the straightedge razor. Mom said I handled it gracefully and my brothers called me Grace for years.

219

I did not go home wearing the crown, but I was first runner-up. Mom knew one of the judges, who told her I only lost by one point. I wasn't a good sport and ran to Craig with tears in my eyes.

"I wanted to win more than anything. I let you down," I said.

"You could never let me down. You should have won, you were robbed," Craig said, with his arms around me.

Miss Yolo County was a student who attended the University of California at Davis and lived in the San Francisco Bay Area. She was a gorgeous brunette and the night of the opening of the State Fair, she won the Maid of California Pageant. The following morning, the *Sacramento Bee* ran a story detailing her past arrest for grand theft. She had been arrested as a juvenile and put on probation and the pageant rules stated that girls entering the pageant could not have been convicted of any crime. I guess she didn't read the rules. To make matters worse, after her arrest was made public, she was allowed to compete for Miss California at the state pageant in Los Angeles and she didn't even make the top 10. Served her right.

The story ran in all the local newspapers and the pageant seemed like a joke. I was asked to fill in for her as the first runner-up.

"Mom, do I have to go to that event and represent Yolo County? Everyone knows what happened and it makes me look like an idiot."

"No, it makes her look like an idiot. You are the first runner-up. You walk into that event with your head held high. You have nothing to be ashamed of."

The whole pageant business left a bad taste in my mouth. The moment was gone and I would never know what it was like to stand on the stage in front of my family and be crowned Miss Yolo County. I didn't want to stand in for a girl who had lied and won. I made one appearance and that was that.

Craig came to the farm during the summer to hunt with Dad. I was in love with him. He was a good guy and could handle my large, loud, overbearing family. Bringing a boy home to meet the family could end the relationship before it started. Family gatherings of thirty people were hectic with kids running around screaming, teasing one another and fighting. It was hard to get a word in edgewise and a lot for anyone to deal with.

When Mom hosted family dinners, we were exhausted by the time everyone went home. Mom knew how to put on a party and organize the pandemonium, but cleaning up the mess and doing the dishes took hours. It was a good time though, and Craig fit in.

Craig's family was small and their dinners were quiet and boring. His mother and sisters judged me. I loved Craig's Dad; he was like my Dad—salt of the earth, kind, generous and nonjudgmental. Craig's Dad didn't come from money, and worked hard to make a better life for his family than he had, just like my Dad.

When school started in the fall, Joe was quarterback of the varsity football team and I came home from college to watch him play. The team had a winning season because of Joe, and Dad could barely contain himself at the games, sitting in the bleachers with the other parents on Friday evenings as the town lit up from the glow of the stadium lights. Not only was Joe smart, he was fast and strong, and one cool quarterback. Donna came home for Joe's games too. She was a student at UCD and sitting at the kitchen table in the house after one of Joe's games, we were trading stories about college and boys who behaved badly.

"Still going out with Bill?" I asked.

"No, he's disappeared. Not sure if he had another girlfriend...or a boyfriend."

"I thought he was weird anyway."

"Well, you won't believe what happened last weekend," Donna said, and started to laugh.

"With Bill?"

"Oh my God, no. With Cindy and her mom."

"Didn't you and Cindy and your friends go to San Francisco?"

"Yes, and the girls drank too much. I was the designated driver and Cindy got sick and threw up all the way across the Golden Gate Bridge," Donna laughed.

"What's so funny about that?"

"The next morning Mom and I went to town and stopped by Cindy's house to give her the sweater she left in my car. She and her Mom were sitting in the kitchen and Cindy was hungover and looked like shit. Her Mom was giving her a bad time and I couldn't resist."

"What are you talking about?" I asked, laughing at Donna laughing at herself.

"Mom and I sat down with them to have a cup of coffee and Mom said, 'Did you girls have a good time last night?' So I said, 'We had a great time, but the girls drank too much and Cindy blew chow all the way across the Golden Gate Bridge.' Cindy's mom looks at me, and then at Cindy and said, 'Who's Chow?' I thought Mom and I were going to die laughing. Even Cindy cracked up. We had to explain the whole thing to her mom. She thought Cindy was in the backseat with some guy named Chow. We laughed for an hour. You should have been there, it was hysterical."

"Where did Mom and Dad say they were going after Joe's game tonight?"

"To the late movie. They won't be home for a couple of hours," Donna replied, as a car slowly pulled into the driveway to the back door. "Who's that? I can't tell whose car it is."

"It's Joe. He's got someone with him."

"It must be a girl. What's he doing home? I thought he was going to the dance after the game."

"No, it's not a girl, it's a guy," I said, as we watched them get out of the car. Joe stumbled and grabbed the car door.

"They're drunk. He can hardly stand up," Donna said.

"Joe, Mr. Football, drunk? I didn't know he drank," I said, as I walked to the back door and turned on the light. Joe and Vaughn came stumbling to the kitchen door. "Oh my God, you are drunk."

"I thought you were going to the dance? Where did you get the liquor?" Donna asked. "It's a good thing Mom and Dad aren't home. Dad would kick your ass. Joe, are you all right?"

Joe grabbed the kitchen chair. "Don't feel good. Going to bed," he slurred.

"I'm going to be sick," Vaughn said.

I followed them to the bedroom. They closed the door and I heard them falling, bumping into the furniture.

"Well, that's a first," I said, as I walked back to the kitchen.

"No it's not," Donna said. "It's not the first time Joe's been drunk after a game. He got his license taken away for six months and just got it back. Guess no one told you."

"I thought I was the only one around here that drank and got in trouble; no wonder Mom and Dad didn't tell me. I'm sure they didn't want me to find out. Guess Joe isn't Mr. Perfect after all. Probably a good thing Dan stayed at a friend's house tonight."

"He knows Joe got caught drinking and had his license taken away. Dan gave Joe such a bad time, they got into a big fight about it. I think Joe was embarrassed in front of his little brother."

Just then another car pulled into the driveway.

"Shit, it's Mom and Dad. What are they doing home? They said they were going to the late movie," Donna said.

"Don't say anything. Dad will be upset."

"I'm not going to say a word," Donna said. "Mom. Dad." You're home early," as they walked into the kitchen.

"The movie had started by the time we got there. It's probably a good thing. It was full of sex," Mom whispered, as she bent over toward Donna and me. "Your father didn't want to stay. What is Joe doing home so early? I thought he was going out with Vaughn after the game? Don't tell me they're in bed already?"

"Yeah," Donna said. "Think they had enough excitement for one night." She looked at me and rolled her eyes.

"You kids have a good night. I'm turning in," Dad said. As Dad uttered those words, we heard a loud crash in the hallway.

"What's that? I thought the boys were in bed. Sounded like someone fell down," Dad said, as he walked down the hallway.

The bedroom door was open and the room was black. The bathroom door was closed and we heard another crash.

"It must be Vaughn in the bathroom throwing up," I whispered to Donna.

Dad pounded on the bathroom door.

"What's going on in there?" Silence. Dad grabbed the doorknob and opened the door.

Joe was puking his guts out. Dad never said a word. He bent down, picked Joe up by the shirt around his neck, dragged him to the shower, opened the door, threw him in clothes and all, and turned on the cold water.

"Shit, let go of me!" Joe hollered, his arms flailing in the air.

"What the hell do you think you're doing? Clean yourself up and go to bed!" Dad said, slamming the door.

"Did you girls buy Joe the beer?" Dad said, in a loud voice.

"No way. We had nothing to do with this. Where would I get the beer? I'm not old enough to buy it," Donna said.

"That's never stopped you girls before," Dad said.

I knew from experience that Joe was in deep shit. Mom and Dad were strict with me, always telling me to set a good example for my sister and brothers. When I didn't, they made an example out of me. They took away the car and grounded me. But Joe wasn't grounded after his little escapade and Dad didn't take away his car. How would

Joe get to football practice? Mom and Dad weren't as strict with the boys as they were with me. I introduced Mom and Dad to what kids were doing in high school and my parents became more tolerant, accepting and reasonable as time went on.

Joe got his first car when he was 16 and I had to wait until I went to college. I wasn't allowed to go on a date with a boy in his car until I was a junior and Donna got to when she was a freshman. That happens when you're the oldest; you end up being the guinea pig.

Craig and Me, 1973

Chapter 19

It was a trip none of us would forget.

Dad had talked about traveling through Canada and Alaska since I was a kid, and I'd be a senior in college in the fall. When harvest was over, he bought a camper that slept four people that attached to the back of his pickup and off we went with what we needed for a six-week road trip in the wilderness. The four of us kids slept in the camper and Mom and Dad pitched a tent and some nights slept under the stars in their sleeping bag.

"This is the trip of a lifetime," Dad said.

Six people in a pickup camper, we'll be on top of one another for six weeks with nowhere to escape, I thought.

Dad woke up before six every morning and threw his double sleeping bag in the back of the camper with us kids still sleeping. By 9 a.m., we were dressed and ate breakfast along the route Dad mapped out. We drove through Glacier National Park before crossing into Canada to attend the Calgary Stampede, a rodeo spectacle none of us had ever experienced. Then on to Lake Louise, Banff National Park and Jasper National Park—untouched landscapes of extreme beauty. This was Dad's dream trip and we were going to enjoy it. Or else.

"It's the least you can do for your father after everything he's done for you," Mom said. "Your Dad has thought about this trip and planned it for years and I want you to get along and make your Dad happy."

Even if I have to spend my 21st birthday with my family in the middle of nowhere.

Dad drove and drove and drove and loved every minute and called the farm every few days to check in. We traveled through Alberta, British Columbia and the Yukon Territory on freeways, backcountry roads, and gravel trails with chuckholes the size of pickup tires. The landscape was vast with rolling hills, valleys, meadows of wildflowers, mountain ranges, forests, rivers, lakes and one small town after another. During meals there wasn't enough room in the camper to move around and things got a little testy. The first few days we were glued to the windows to look at the scenery, but after a while the country looked the same. The four of us kids spent hours in the back of the camper playing cards and table games and Dad didn't understand.

"Look," Dad yelled, pointing out the window. "Look at the size of those redwood trees. Kids, you're missing all the best stuff. You'll never see forests like this again."

"Promise?" Donna asked, under her breath.

We fished, kayaked, swam, hiked, ate, laughed and fought. We collected rocks, dried flowers, pine cones and bags full of stuff that ended up in the garbage. When we got to Fairbanks, Alaska, Joe, Dan and Dad flew to the backcountry in a private plane to fish on a lake accessible only by air. They came back with white faces and upset stomachs.

"The airstrip was next to the lake, if you want to call it an airstrip," Joe said. "When the pilot dove the plane to land, he almost dumped us into the lake, and we had to circle and come back around."

"That's not true," Dad said. "He hit the lake."

"I thought we were goners," Dan said. "We were headed straight into the water and I couldn't see the landing strip. When we got out of the plane, the wheels were sitting in the lake."

"That's the last time I'm doing that," Joe said.

"Me too," Dan said.

"Where's the fish?" Mom asked.

There was a long silence.

"The pilot almost hit the lake coming to pick us up. We got nervous and left the fish behind," Dan said. "We caught so many fish we could barely pick up the sack. The last thing we needed was more weight in the plane."

Mom, Donna and I looked at each other and cracked up.

So much for the boys never getting in a private plane again. The next morning we flew to Barrow at the northernmost tip of Alaska and the only way to get there was in a private plane. The sun never set and we were surrounded by ice and snow as far as we could see. I thought Eskimos lived in igloos, but I didn't see any igloos. We rode a dogsled pulled by eight Alaskan huskies that looked like wolves, and traveled across snow and tundra until we came to a village with igloos. The Eskimos didn't live in the igloos though; the igloos were just for show.

That night we celebrated my 21st birthday in the only restaurant in town, eating caribou, reindeer and the local delicacy, whale blubber. The blubber was cut into tiny, black-and-white miniature squares, stuck on the ends of toothpicks, and tasted like stinky rubber. I didn't want to hurt the Eskimos' feelings, but I couldn't eat it. When we went to bed at midnight it was light outside.

"How many kids can say they turned twenty-one at the North Pole?" Dad asked. "Not many, I bet."

"I bet you're right, Dad," I said.

It was a birthday I will never forget.

Mt. McKinley stood out above the clouds from Anchorage, rising up into the clear blue sky, glistening and covered in snow. After driving around Prince William Sound, Dad drove the camper onto the ferry in Haines Junction in the Yukon and we rode down the coast of Alaska on the Alaska Highway with Dad seasick most of the time, hanging over the rails throwing up. Skagway, Juneau, Sitka and Prince Rupert, where we all bought handsewn mucklucks made from beaver and fox. On to Vancouver, Victoria, Busch Gardens and the Olympic Brewing Company, where I had my first beer, legally.

After six weeks we headed back to California. We couldn't wait to get in our beds and take a hot shower. Our clothes were dirty, the sleeping bags were smelly and damp, the fridge stunk, and we'd eaten enough bologna sandwiches to last a lifetime. Our last day on the road we stopped for lunch and Donna was talking back to Mom. They got into a doozie of an argument.

"You will not talk to me like that, young lady," Mom said.

"I will talk to you however I want," Donna said.

"You will not," Mom said, shaking her finger at Donna, as Donna pushed Mom.

"That's enough. Everybody in. It's time to go home," Dad said, as he stood in the middle of the two of them. Dad drove to the farm without stopping.

We talked about the trip to Alaska for years. We still talk about it and Dad remembers it like it was yesterday. The stories get longer and funnier depending on whose exaggerated tale one chooses to believe.

I sent Craig a postcard every day from the road. We were graduating the following June. Craig was a junior when we met and I was a freshman. He came to college to party and have fun. I came to college to get a degree and a husband. I wanted to get married and have a family, just like Mom and Dad. Craig asked me to marry him at Christmas and I said yes. The first person I called was Virginia.

"Craig asked me to marry him," I said, my voice full of excitement.

"I'm happy for you. I know this is what you've always wanted."

"Do you remember the first day of college when I pointed him out at the milk machine and told you I was going to marry him?"

"Yes, I remember. Better be careful what you wish for." We laughed with the same breath.

Craig wasn't a Catholic and didn't go to church and Dad told me if Craig wouldn't marry me in the Catholic Church, I couldn't marry him. I never had to tell Craig that; he knew I went to church every Sunday and he agreed to marry me in the church where I grew up. My faith had a profound effect on me and influenced how I lived my life and Craig knew that.

Following graduation, Craig and I made plans to marry in November. I was marrying the man of my dreams and planned a church wedding with 300 guests at St. Anthony's. I was following in my parents' footsteps and wanted what they had: a solid marriage, love, respect and children. I wanted to live my life as my parents had lived theirs and would raise my children the way they raised me. I was starting a new life with my husband, away from my home, my family and the farm, and moving to Turlock where Craig would work in his father's business.

Donna was attending UCD and studying to be a nurse. Joe was a senior and star quarterback on the football team at Winters High School and Dan was a freshman. Joe was big man on campus that year and I know Dan looked up to his brother. But Joe and Dan were as different as they could be. Joe was a perfectionist and competitive and wanted things to be his way, pretty much like Dad. Dan was easygoing, went along with what others wanted to do and things didn't always have to be perfect. Both of them were sure good looking though. Joe reminded me of John Kennedy, Jr., and Dan looked like a young Robert Redford. I had a feeling that once Joe graduated, Dan would come into his own and excel. I was right. Being the oldest, I could only imagine what it was like for Dan to try and keep up with his older siblings and first cousins who tried to be the best at everything.

Winters won the sectional championship and Joe was selected Northern California Small School Quarterback of the Year. He played in the East-West Shrine Game in Sacramento and his team won. I cut every article out of the local papers, saved every ticket, and made a scrapbook for his graduation, when he was also valedictorian of his class. We were all proud of Joe when he got accepted to Stanford.

New Holland hay swather, circa 1970s

Chapter 20

November was just six months away.

Mom and I were busy making wedding plans, but Dad had plans of his own and put me in charge of swathing alfalfa for the summer. The swather resembled a gigantic lawn mower with an air-conditioned cab that sat up off the ground a few feet. Across the front of the machine was a 15-foot header, concealing a blade that moved swiftly from side to side, cutting the hay inches above the ground. A circular shaft fed the cut hay into the swather and onto a conveyor belt that moved the alfalfa to the back of the machine, where it fell to the ground in three-foot-wide windrows.

When swathing alfalfa, the first thing to do is "head out" the field. To "head out" a field means swathing three rows around the field's perimeter, which then allows room for making turns once you begin cutting the alfalfa in straight rows from one end of the field to the other.

Dad always gave me instructions when he taught me to drive a new piece of equipment. "When you work around farm equipment, do not wear jewelry, or rings, you could lose a finger. Don't wear loose clothing and don't leave that long hair of yours untied. Best to tuck it under a hat."

"Got it, Dad. You've told me that a million times."

I woke up late one morning and hurried to get out of the house. I wouldn't have overslept if Dad had been home—he'd have had a hissy fit—so it was a good thing Mom and Dad were at Dillon Beach. I threw on my jeans and work shirt and put my long hair in braids and ran to the alfalfa field next to Grandma's house. The mechanic had just finished fueling up the swather.

Shit, I thought, *he'll tell Dad I was late for work.* "Morning. Don't worry about greasing the chains. I have oil in the cab."

Not only did Dad teach all of us how to drive, he taught us how to fuel the farm equipment and oil the parts.

"If you're going to drive the equipment you better know how to service it. I don't want you blowing up the engine," Dad had said, over and over.

I jumped in the cab and turned on the motor, put the swather in neutral, set the brake and climbed down the ladder with the oilcan. I slid under the machine and began lubricating the chains that circled above my head until they moved easily. As I started to slide out from under the machine, pulling myself along the ground with my hands, I heard a clanging sound and turned to see where the noise was coming from.

As I tossed my head, my long braid caught in the moving chain and my head slammed backwards. My neck cracked. I was caught. My braid was in the machine and my head was being pulled into the motor. In a matter of seconds, I was free, but only because my hair was ripped off my head. My life flashed in front of me: I saw kids on the merry-go-round at Union School and Grandpa milking the cow. I didn't know what happened. Then I saw my braid stuck in the chain and felt like I was in the shower. I put my hands to my head and my face and my hands were covered in blood. Blood was everywhere, running down my face like water. I slumped over and sunk my fingers in the dirt, pulling myself out from under the swather as I stood up, dazed.

Bob, one of the farmworkers, saw what happened, pulled the pickup next to the swather and swung open the door. I collapsed on the front seat. The next thing I knew Grandma opened the pickup door, screamed and fainted, and Aunt Claire jumped in with a pillow and blanket. She wrapped a towel around my head as we raced to the hospital twenty miles away. Things were a blur.

"Aunt Claire, am I going to be OK?"

"Can you tell me your phone number?"

I told her our number. "You're going to be fine. Lie still and don't talk. We'll be at the hospital soon," she said, with my head bleeding in her lap.

Bob was driving eighty miles an hour when a Highway Patrol pulled us over, and Bob said the officer took one look at me and escorted us to the hospital. I never lost consciousness and didn't feel pain until after the X-rays when the doctor started to stitch my scalp back together.

"You're one lucky girl. You're lucky to be alive," the doctor said. "I put more than a hundred stitches in your head."

My scalp looked like a road map. The hair was torn from my head and the pressure from my hair being pulled out had ripped the skin from my skull. I had been in the hospital two hours when Mom and Dad ran into the emergency room. They looked scared to death. They had been at the beach, where there was no telephone. Aunt Claire had to notify the police, who went to the cabin and knocked on the door.

Dad remembered the tragic accident of one of his friend's sons, who was working on a tractor in the field when the gust from the tractor fan blew off his hat. His long hair caught in the fan, and his son was scalped in the field and bled to death before anyone came to help him.

The swather had pulled the hair off my own head like a swim cap. That was a good thing, or my head would have been crushed in the motor. My bottom lip was sliced open on the inside, hanging down on my chin, and several of my teeth were broken and chipped, and my jaw was cracked, but the rest of my face didn't have a mark on it. Like the doctor said, I was lucky.

"I'm not going to keep her overnight," the doctor said. "She needs to see an oral surgeon right away. I called and he's waiting in his office. Several of her teeth are broken and she has a cracked jaw. I've given her morphine. You'll need to bring her back in a day or two so

I can lance her head to drain the blood that's going to collect under her scalp. Keep an eye on her tonight. Her head will swell like a basketball and her eyes will swell shut. Call me if you have any problems."

"Are you sure we should take her home today?" Mom said.

"I'll keep her here for another hour. I doubt the oral surgeon will do anything today, but he needs to take a look at her."

Aunt Claire called Craig when we got to the hospital and he walked in and heard the doctor talking. When I saw the look on Craig's face, I knew I was a mess.

"You're going to be all right," he said, as his voice cracked. He grabbed my hand. His face was white as a ghost and I thought he was going to faint.

"Your jaw is cracked and your mouth is cut up. There isn't much I can do today," the oral surgeon said. "Try not to talk. Drink out of a straw and no solid foods. You have ten teeth that are broken and will need root canals. Come back in a few days and we'll take more X-rays and decide what to do first."

Mom and Dad insisted I sleep in their king-size bed and have their room to myself. I passed out from the pain medicine and slept for a day. When I woke up, Dad was sitting by the bed staring at me.

"When the officer knocked on the beach cabin door and told me what happened to you, all I could think about was my friend's son." His voice cracked. "I thought we were going to lose you. We jumped in the car and raced home as fast as we could and didn't even pack our stuff. You didn't tie your hair back, did you?"

"No, Dad. I overslept. I was in a hurry."

"Your grandmother is convinced you didn't die because the Good Lord was watching over you. Yesterday was a holy day, the Feast of the Assumption."

"That sounds like something Grandma would say."

Dad bent over and put his face next to mine. "I'm glad you're alive." He pulled back and smiled, shook his head and let out a sigh of relief.

The next morning I woke up and everything was black. "Mom, can you come in here? I can't see."

"Honey, don't get upset. Your head is full of blood and your eyes are swollen shut. The doctor said this was going to happen. We're going to the hospital."

When I sat up, the blood under my skin rolled to the front of my face and my face swelled. When I lay down, the blood rolled to the back of my head and I felt like I was lying in a pillow of water; it was the strangest sensation. The doctor made a small incision in the back of my head behind my ear and drained the blood from under my scalp.

"You need to come in every day for a week," he said. "Keep ice on your eyes and the swelling will go down."

My cousins came by to check on me. The accident had happened so fast that no one turned off the swather. Charlie drove by the swather right after Bob picked me up and figured something was terribly wrong when he saw my braid in the chain and blood on the ground. He came by the house to ask me if I wanted my braid. At first, I said no, but I'm glad I kept it.

For the next week I took painkillers and slept most of the time, except for my daily trip to the hospital and Craig's daily calls to check on me. He lived two hours away and came to visit on the weekends. As the days went by, the pain passed, the swelling went down and I could see again.

"Mom, I'm going in the bathroom and look in the mirror."

"I'm not sure that's a good idea. I don't want you to get upset."

Boy, I thought, *I must look pretty scary.*

I didn't recognize myself. My face was purple and black and the whites of my eyes were bright red. My head was shaped like a gigantic balloon with no indentations around my features and I didn't know whether to laugh or cry. There was baby fuzz on the right side of my head and a long braid on the other. My lips were swollen and scabs covered the top of my head. It was the beginning of September and there was no way I was getting married in November.

"Mom, look at me."

"I told you not to go in the bathroom and look at yourself. It looks much worse than it is. It's going to take time."

"We wasted money on the invitations for the wedding. I can't walk down the aisle in less than two months. Look at me; I can barely open my mouth. Besides that, I'm going to spend the next two months in the dentist chair."

"I think we need to postpone the wedding for a few months."

"Do you think Craig is going to marry me looking like this?"

I moved back into my bedroom after two weeks. I had lost fifteen pounds.

"Better be careful what you wish for," Donna said. "Remember you wanted to lose ten pounds before your wedding. Well, *voila*, you got your wish. Only you had to lose your hair and get the shit kicked out of you to do it."

"Shut up. The last thing I need is your two cents."

My mouth healed enough in a couple of weeks for the oral surgeon to start the root canals and I dreaded every day in the dentist chair. The root canals took over a month.

"Virginia and April called today," Mom said. "They want to come see you and I told them I thought you'd love the company."

"Boy, are they in for a surprise."

Virginia and April were my college roommates and two of my closest friends. When the doorbell rang I went to the door and none of us said a word. They stared at me with their mouths wide open. *If they think I look bad now,* I thought, *they should have seen me a month ago.*

238

April spoke first. "Did you get the number of the tractor that ran over your face?"

I looked at April and then at Virginia. They looked at each other, looked back at me and started laughing.

"Shut up," I said, as I laughed at them laughing at me. "It hurts too much to laugh."

"Are you still getting married in November?" Virginia asked.

"No. We're waiting until February and I still want you to be a bridesmaid in my wedding, and yes, Craig still wants to marry me."

"Has he seen you?" April asked. "Does he know he's marrying the bride of Frankenstein?" They couldn't stop laughing.

"He knows I look like a monster. He came to the hospital. The wedding is definitely on for February."

"You know we're just happy to see you and relieved that you're going to be all right," Virginia said. "Why don't you cut off that long braid; you'll look great with short hair."

I looked ridiculous with baby fuzz on one side of my head and a long braid on the other. The stitches on the top and back of my head were hidden from sight, but I knew I looked frightening. After a few weeks the bruising started to go away, but the whites of my eyes stayed red for months. Everyone told me how lucky I was, how much worse it could have been. I knew I was lucky to be alive, and the fact that I had cuts on my lips and in my mouth, but not on my face, was a miracle.

Mom kept telling me, "God was watching out for you, honey. Be thankful. You could have been permanently injured."

"Yeah," Joe said, laughing, "you could be a vegetable."

"Joe, don't talk to your sister like that," Mom said. "What a terrible thing to say."

My hair wasn't growing back and I was getting married in two months. I couldn't walk down the aisle with shorter hair than my husband-to-be, and he had short hair.

"Mom, I need a wig. Not one of those cheap, shiny fake ones from the drugstore. A real-hair wig."

"We'll call the insurance broker. Your Dad thinks they'll pay for a wig."

The wig was not covered by our insurance and the answer was no. Dad made an appointment with the adjuster and marched me over to the insurance office. I wore a scarf to cover the scars and my half-bald head. The hair follicles were damaged and the doctor wasn't sure my hair would ever grow back.

"Lorraine, Mr. Rominger, how nice to see you. Please have a seat," the adjuster said.

"I understand the insurance company has denied our request for a real-hair wig for my daughter."

"Yes, Mr. Rominger. That's correct. It's not a normal request."

"Well, this is not a normal situation. I think you should reconsider."

There was silence.

"Are you aware that the New Holland swather my daughter was operating didn't have protective shields on the chains? The company removed them because the alfalfa got caught in the shield, clogging up the machine. Maybe I should contact a lawyer and see what he thinks. My daughter has no hair on one side of her head because it was caught and ripped out in a machine that should have had safety shields in place. Lorraine, take off your scarf."

I removed the scarf and leaned my head down over the adjuster's desk. Dad said the adjuster pulled his head back with a sick look on his face.

"I wonder what a judge would say about our request. My daughter needs a wig to walk down the aisle, don't you think?"

"Well, Mr. Rominger. Let me look into it and see what I can do."

"Good," Dad said.

When we got in the car, Dad said he had no intention of getting a lawyer and filing a lawsuit against New Holland. Dad said people were "sue happy" in this country and he was not that kind of person.

The next day the insurance representative for New Holland called and told Dad they'd cover the cost of the real-hair wig. Due to the circumstances, they'd make an exception. A rep for the company came to our house to interview me and ask questions about the accident. He agreed that they would pay my medical and dental expenses, buy two wigs and pay me a salary for the months I was unable to work. All I had to do was sign a document saying I wouldn't sue them in the future. Dad and I signed the papers.

When the doctor said I could go back to work, Dad took me out to the field and insisted I drive the swather, just like the day I broke my leg riding Lady and Dad brought me home from the hospital in a cast and made me ride my horse. It was a long time before I could drive the swather without seeing my braid going round and round stuck in the chain of the motor.

St. Anthony's Catholic Church, 1974

Chapter 21

1974

Moving our wedding from November to February took a little maneuvering.

We lost our deposits, but Mom said it was a small price to pay.

My life was changing and I was leaving the farm, the place I called home for more than twenty years. I would have a husband to take care of now. At our wedding rehearsal the night before the ceremony, I did regret Craig's hair was longer than mine. The insurance company had paid for a beautiful long, softly curled, brunette real-hair wig. But the cathedral-length wedding veil I borrowed from Mom was so heavy it pulled the wig right off my head as I walked down the aisle.

"Thank God I practiced wearing this tonight, Mom," I said laughing, with the wig in my hand. "Do you have any idea how embarrassed I would have been in a church full of people if my wig had fallen off?"

"It won't matter. No one is going to notice your hair. You're going to look beautiful in that wedding dress holding your father's arm."

The next afternoon as Dad drove me to the church, I turned my head for one last glimpse of the farm and the row crops that lined the fields where I grew up.

Craig and I got married at High Mass in the same church where my parents had been married twenty-four years earlier. Joe was an usher in his tuxedo and walked Mom down the aisle in her long, stunning, gold-tailored dress and matching jacket. Donna was my maid of honor, and like my five bridesmaids, wore a long, pale orange, crepe gown. Dan was an altar boy in his white robe with my cousin Matt and of course, Dad, looking ever so handsome in his tuxedo, walked me down the aisle. All of my cousins helped with the wedding. Two of my youngest cousins were the flower girl and ring bearer. Ruth was a bridesmaid and Shannon, Diana and Corinne wore long matching dresses to attend the guestbook and pass out rice bags and groom's cake. Rick, Charlie and Bruce made sculptured metal candleholders that decorated the tables at the country club where we held the sit-down dinner-dance. All my grandparents sat in the front row with my parents and both my Grandpas had on ties I had made them for Christmas. I remember looking at their faces, so happy and so proud. Holding on to my Dad's arm to "Here Comes the Bride," I walked down the aisle shaking with tears running down my face. It was one of the best moments of my life.

I knew I had become who I was because of my parents, my siblings and my grandparents, because of the way I was raised, because of the land that was such an important part of my life. I respected my family for their hard work and resounding faith. They had given me my sense of self, and the farm and the land had given me a sense of place. Growing up on the farm in a house at the end of the lane, I had been given a childhood I would never forget—a way of life I had no idea how much I was going to miss.

Craig and Me, on our wedding day, 1974,
with Popo and Momo Cody on the left,
Grandma and Grandpa Rominger on the right

Mom and Dad, on their wedding day, 1950,
with Popo and Momo Cody on the left,
Grandma and Grandpa Rominger on the right

Cody, James, Eleanore, Dad, Natalie, Julia,
Justine and David, my nieces and nephews,
with their grandfather, 2009

Epilogue

It's been over forty years since I moved away from the farm in 1974, and since then much has happened. My family has had our share of ups and downs, successes and failures, triumphs and tragedies. My siblings and cousins married, had babies, and have families of their own now.

I regret to say my marriage to Craig lasted ten years. We didn't have children and I always thought I'd have a houseful of kids. I never stopped loving him and we didn't part enemies, but we grew apart, and when I look back, we were young and immature and gave up too easily. When he died of Hodgkin's disease at 39, I was devastated, and had spent as much time with him as I could when he was in and out of the hospital. I have a great deal of faith and attend mass every Sunday, but after Craig died I didn't go to church for months. I know it wasn't God's fault, but I prayed to God to save him.

I did not remarry and I thank heaven every day for my nieces and nephews: Julia, David, Justine, Cody, Eleanore, James and Natalie, who have become the joys of my life. I am so proud of each one of them. My oldest niece, Julia, married Mackenzie, and I have two adorable great-nieces, Mahea and Noelle. My nieces and nephews are one of the reasons I wrote this book, to share the traditions and rituals passed down by our family for generations.

There were things I took for granted growing up that are gone now, things my nieces and nephews will not have the opportunity to experience, like the simplicity of a farm family whose life revolved around a place where we lived and worked, so our family and farm would prosper. Dad's attachment to the land, and his father's, is like none any of us will know. My grandparents have passed, but Dad and Grandpa Rominger have collectively been on the farm for nearly a century and have witnessed the wild, open country be taken away over time. I prefer that world I grew up in, not the world I am growing old in.

I was living in New York in November 2000 when I received the call from Donna that Mom had a glioblastoma, the most aggressive of brain tumors, and was having surgery in two days. The flight from New York to the farm took six hours, but it seemed like six days. Mom went through hell, but she never complained or felt sorry for herself. Her only worry was for her family and how Dad was going to get by. When she died the day after Christmas, our world collapsed. As my Dad carried my naked mother to her bed after she had stopped breathing in the shower, I realized I'd never seen my Dad cry. Mom was a remarkable woman with deep faith and bravery beyond belief. I hope I can be that brave when I face the end of my life.

Four hundred people came to Mom's funeral at St. Anthony's Catholic Church, spilling out onto the sidewalk. A few months later the new school in Winters was named Shirley Rominger Intermediate School. My parents knew most everyone in town and were loved and respected by all, and it was a huge honor for my Mom and our family. Dad could barely speak at the dedication, a day my family will always remember. Mom is the other reason I wrote this book, to pay tribute to her and Dad for the legacy they preserve and continue.

After Mom's funeral we planted a willow branch from one of the funeral arrangements in front of the house, which has grown to be the largest tree in the yard. Sometimes when the wind blows I feel it's Mom rustling through the branches looking out for all of us. Even in her absence I feel her influence and she continues to shape our lives. Mom's death gave me a purpose in life I didn't have before.

Every year on December 26th, my Dad, sister, brothers, nieces and nephews attend mass at St. Anthony's in Mom's honor, visit her gravesite, stand in a circle around her headstone, hand in hand, and pray together. Dad still goes to the cemetery every morning after fifteen years, and you can see his boot prints embedded in the grass. I could never take Mom's place, nor want to, but I will carry on the traditions that have been in our family for generations. I can't expect Dad to do that; men aren't the best at those kind of things. You could say I've taken over for Mom, who was a great teacher, and I feel I've been given the privilege of carrying on a legacy.

I look forward to holidays, birthdays, soccer and volleyball games, swim meets, school plays and graduations when all of our family gets together. I cook the same meal, bake the same chocolate cake, set the same table and use the same decorations that we used when Mom was alive.

I often wonder what will happen to the farm when my generation is gone. My nieces and nephews didn't work on the farm every summer like we did, or go to school in Winters. They went to grammar school and high school in a neighboring town, and don't feel the same attachment to the land as my generation and my Dad's and Grandpa's. They are interested in doing other things and a life away from the farm. I'm not sure who will take over the place and I don't want our legacy to disappear. My life did revolve around the love of a family and a place that I wouldn't trade for anything, the land I love that has given me a sense of permanence. Being a farmer is not just a job, it is a way of life.

A photo I have from my class at Waggoner Elementary School in 1962, the year I started school in Winters, is representative of the town I called home. Many of the kids in my sixth-grade class still live in Winters. The town is made up of people who embrace the important role of family, the unique experience of small-town life, and the support and love of a close-knit agricultural community. I can't wait to move back to the farm and Winters when I retire. It is where my heart will always be.

Shirley Rominger Intermediate School, dedicated 2001

Acknowledgments

I'd like to thank my family, especially Mom and Dad, for giving me the most wonderful childhood and a safe and loving place to grow up. To my sister, Donna, and my brothers, Joe and Dan, for being there for me; I know I can always count on them. To my grandparents, who I looked up to; they were the best role models. I didn't realize how lucky I was to have a family like mine until I left the farm. And to my nieces and nephews, for the happiness they bring into my life every day.

Special thanks to my writing teacher, Alan Kaufman, for his continual encouragement that pushed me to start writing this book; to my editor, Molly Giles, for caring and showing it; to Sam Barry, head of the Path to Publishing program at Book Passage in the Bay Area, for his guidance; to Jim Shubin, for transforming my manuscript into a book and bringing my old family photos to life; and to my dearest friend, Jennifer Walton, for her keen sense of design, always knowing the answer and sticking with me on this journey.

I can never adequately thank all of my extended family and friends, many of whom I mention in this book and most of whom I don't, for your love and support. All of you have helped me write my story.

About the Author

Lorraine Rominger lives in San Francisco where she manages an international environmental foundation. Most weekends she drives an hour to the farm to visit her family and ride around in the pickup with her Dad and his dog.

Photos

The photos on these few pages were taken between the 1910s and the 1970s.

1. Momo Cody and my Mom
2. Great-Grandma Sara Williams (Momo Cody's Mom)
3. My Mom
4. Me, Mom and Donna
5. Grandma Rominger

6. Aunt Lucille, Grandma Rominger, Aunt Claire and Aunt Joan
7. Mom and me, in our new house
8. Me
9. Auntie Lona and my Mom
10. Great-Grandma Mary Erhardt (Grandma Rominger's Mom)

1. Uncle Richard and my Dad
2. Dan and Joe
3. Great-Grandma Elizabeth Rominger and Great-Grandpa Charles Rominger (on far right) with their 11 children; Grandpa Rominger is standing second from left
4. My Dad
5. Joe and Dan, with my Mom in the background

6. My husband, Craig
7. Joe
8. Grandpa Rominger
9. Popo Cody
10. My Dad
11. Joe and Dan
12. Popo Cody (center back) with his four brothers, Bill, Les, Sam and Mack, and his father, William (center front)

1. Donna, Joe and me
2. Mom, me, Dad and Donna
3. Me and Lady
4. Charlie, me, Rick and Donna
5. Popo and Momo Cody, and Popo's four brothers and their wives
6. Uncle Richard, Aunt Lucille, Aunt Claire, my Dad and Aunt Joan
7. Richard and Mary Washabaugh (my Godparents), Mom (holding me) and Dad, at my baptism

8. My Dad, Aunt Claire, Grandpa Rominger, Aunt Lucille, Grandma Rominger, Aunt Joan and Uncle Richard
9. My Dad, Great-Grandma Mary Erhardt (holding me) and Grandma Rominger—four generations
10. Me, Donna, Charlie and Rick
11. Momo and Popo Cody
12. Uncle Richard, Aunt Lucille, Aunt Claire, Aunt Joan and my Dad, at Dillon Beach
13. Momo and Popo Cody, on their wedding day
14. Our house on the farm

1. Some of our family on the front lawn of the shack, at my baptism
2. Joe on Easter Sunday, with our cousin and uncle in the background
3. Grandma and Grandpa Rominger, on their wedding day
4. Auntie Lona
5. Me
6. Joe, hanging sausage, on the second day of butchering
7. Mom, Auntie Lona and their cousins
8. Me and Donna

9. Me, our cousin and Donna
10. Popo Cody (second from left) with three of his four brothers at school
11. Grandpa Rominger on the tractor
12. My Mom
13. A few of the Rangity Tango Kids, at my wedding
14. My Dad, Mom, Donna, me, Craig, Dan and Joe, on my wedding day

CPSIA information can be obtained at www.ICGtesting.com
Printed in the USA
LVOW11*0317110816

499905LV00006B/13/P